Family Child Care
Guide to Visits,
Inspections, and Interviews

Also from Redleaf Press by Donna C. Hurley and Sharon Woodward

The Home Visitor's Manual: Tools and Strategies for
Effective Interactions with Family Child Care Providers

Also from Redleaf Press by Sharon Woodward

Family Child Care Curriculum: Teaching through Quality Care
Family Child Care Curriculum Family Companion
Family Child Care Curriculum Developmental Assessment Guide

FAMILY CHILD CARE

Guide to Visits, Inspections, and Interviews

DONNA C. HURLEY
SHARON WOODWARD

Redleaf Press®
www.redleafpress.org
800-423-8309

5 0503 01110626 9

Published by Redleaf Press
10 Yorkton Court
St. Paul, MN 55117
www.redleafpress.org

Portions of this book are based on *The Home Visitor's Manual: Tools and Strategies for Effective Interactions with Family Child Care Providers* by Sharon Woodward and Donna C. Hurley. Copyright © 2011 by Sharon Woodward and Donna C. Hurley. Published by Redleaf Press, St. Paul, MN, www.redleafpress.org.

First edition 2013
Cover design by Jim Handrigan
Cover photograph by Veer/Ocean Photography
Interior design by Jim Handrigan
Typeset in Mrs Eaves and Mr Eaves
Printed in the United States of America
20 19 18 17 16 15 14 13   1 2 3 4 5 6 7 8

Library of Congress Cataloging-in-Publication Data
Hurley, Donna C.
   Family child care guide to visits, inspections, and interviews / Donna C. Hurley and Sharon Woodward. — 1st ed.
      p. cm.
   Includes bibliographical references.
   ISBN 978-1-60554-126-6 (pbk. : alk. paper)
   ISBN 978-1-60554-255-3 (e-book)
   1. Family day care—United States. 2. Family day care—United States—Case studies.   I. Woodward, Sharon. II. Title.
   HQ778.63.H87 2013
   362.71'20973—dc23
                    2012043442

Printed on acid-free paper

To a wonderful partnership

CONTENTS

Acknowledgments xi

Introduction xiii

Chapter 1: Lead Your Family-Team 1

Case Study 1: Susan's Family-Team Communication

Challenge: Ensuring Cooperation from Family Members

　　Solution: Create Collaboration

　　Solution: Be Specific about Your Expectations

　　Solution: Empower Your Own Children

Challenge: Maintaining "Visit Ready" Conditions

　　Solution: Create and Use a Visit Ready Checklist

　　Solution: Plan Good Storage Options from the Beginning

Case Study 2: Susan Invites Everyone On Board

Checkpoints for Success

Chapter 2: Think Like a Family Member 13

Case Study 1: Clara's Family Friction

Challenge: Managing Your Family's Involvement on an Ongoing Basis

　　Solution: Focus on the Benefits for All

Challenge: Keeping Clients Happy While Meeting Your Own Goals

　　Solution: Put Your Philosophy and Corresponding Needs in Writing

Challenge: Recruiting New Clients

　　Solution: Present Your Program as a Professional

Case Study 2: Clara Addresses Problems through the Families' Perspectives

Checkpoints for Success

Chapter 3: Be Prepared for Visits 35

Case Study 1: Maria—Unprepared for the Unexpected

Challenge: Dealing with Unforeseen Variables

　　Solution: Stay Current with Regulations

Challenge: Understanding Your Role during Visits

　　Solution: Understand the Goal of Each Type of Visit

Challenge: Effectively Anticipating a Visit

　　Solution: Remain Informed and Up to Date

　　Solution: Care about Yourself

　　Solution: Get Organized

Case Study 2: Maria Is Ready

Checkpoints for Success

Chapter 4: Communicate Effectively 51

    Case Study 1: Carmen's Inability to Speak Up

    Challenge: Presenting Ideas Clearly

        Solution: Match Body Language to Message

        Solution: Interpret Others' Body Language Carefully

    Challenge: Dealing with Different Communication Styles

        Solution: Learn to Recognize and Communicate with Different Styles

        Solution: Know Your Own Communication Style

        Solution: Manage Conflicts between Styles

    Challenge: Listening Effectively

        Solution: Listen Actively

    Case Study 2: Carmen Respectfully Explains Her Ideas

    Checkpoints for Success

Chapter 5: Maintain a Positive Attitude 73

    Case Study 1: Simone's Confrontational Disaster

    Challenge: Handling Confrontations

        Solution: Control Your Responses

        Solution: Respond Effectively to Passive-Aggressive Behavior

    Challenge: Remaining Assertive

        Solution: Turn Confrontations into Collaborations

        Solution: Be Aware of How You Are Coming Across

        Solution: Use Assertive Language

    Challenge: Understanding Others' Points of View

        Solution: Show That You Value What Others Say

    Challenge: Trying to Predict How Interactions Might Go

        Solution: Focus on Your Intended Outcomes

        Solution: Use Documentation to Your Advantage

    Challenge: Maintaining an Appropriate Balance of Authority

        Solution: Stand Up for Yourself

    Case Study 2: Simone Plans to Accomplish Goals and Prevent Disasters

    Checkpoints for Success

Chapter 6: Participate Fully in Visits 95

    Case Study 1: Karen and John Distractedly Receive Visitors

    Challenge: Making Visits an Interactive Process

        Solution: Document What Happens

        Solution: Control the Tempo of the Visit

        Solution: Achieve a Balance of Authority during Your Professional Interactions

    Challenge: Remaining Focused throughout a Visit

        Solution: Concentrate on Taking Notes

        Solution: Prepare Children in Advance for Visitors

    Case Study 2: Karen and John Concentrate on Inspector Visits

    Checkpoints for Success

Chapter 7: Follow-Up 107

    Case Study 1: Kay's Confidence Is Uninformed

    Challenge: Responding to Issues When They Are Raised

        Solution: Take Every Communication Seriously

        Solution: Regularly Check on Your Status

    Challenge: Deciding What to Own

        Solution: Take the Lessons You Teach Children to Heart

    Challenge: Understanding Regulations and Citations

        Solution: Be Persistent until You Have Clarification

    Challenge: Responding to Citations and/or Legal Orders Appropriately

        Solution: Give a Rebuttal or Make Corrections Immediately

        Solution: Pay Attention to Deadlines

        Solution: Respond Appropriately

    Challenge: Ensuring Information Made Available to the Public Is Correct

        Solution: Stay Up to Date on How Your State Shares Information

    Case Study 2: Kay Is Confident and Knowledgeable

    Checkpoints for Success

ACKNOWLEDGMENTS

We would like to thank Kyra Ostendorf of Redleaf Press for her support and enthusiasm, as well as Deanne Kells for her patience and thoughtful editing.

We would also like to extend a special thank you to all of the family child care providers who have shared their concerns and perspectives in ways that consistently reflect their commitment to quality child care.

To the Family Child Care Association of New York State, we would like to say thank you for inviting us to present at your conference. The discussions that first took place there were the genesis of this book.

Lastly, we would like to extend our appreciation to the children in our lives who inspire us to help make child care as rewarding an experience as possible. Thank you to Benjamin, Cole, Luca, and Ellie. Our sincere gratitude to Richie and Ryan, Josh and Michael, Alleyah and Martin, Wilson, Amari, Javien, and Mia.

INTRODUCTION

We have collectively worked in the field of early childhood education for more than eighty years. Our backgrounds include experiences as child care providers, licensors, child care administrators, and trainers. We are pleased to welcome you to the *Family Child Care Guide to Visits, Inspections, and Interviews*.

Who This Manual Is For

While traveling throughout the United States to make presentations at state and national conferences, we have met hundreds of individuals who provide services from their homes. From talking to you, we know that you might be visited because you receive Child and Adult Care Food Program (CACFP) food reimbursement funds or a subsidy for care of income-eligible children. You might also be visited by Head Start and early intervention personnel; fire, building, and health and safety inspectors; mentors; Child Development Associate (CDA) monitors; licensors; accreditation and environmental rating scale observers; and potential clients. Therefore, this book is written for your reference when you have people visit your home for a variety of purposes:

- inspection
- monitoring
- evaluation
- support
- accountability
- technical assistance
- investigation
- assessment of your services

Why We Wrote This Manual

As providers caring for children, you have the most important job in the world: loving, nurturing, teaching, and guiding young children during their most formative and vulnerable years. When planning and operating your child care business, you attend to

- **the children:** their health, safety, and developmental needs
- **the families of the children:** their needs and demands (requests about naptime, discipline, payment schedules, siblings, and TV watching, to name just a few)
- **your own family:** their schedules, feelings of jealousy, need for personal time with you
- **business operation:** financial, budgeting, scheduling, marketing, and regulatory requirements

All of these are important parts of your business plan, and you address them with amazing patience and insight.

In talking with hundreds of providers across the United States, we have learned that many of you have questions, comments, frustrations, and strong opinions about how to handle the representatives who visit your homes for the purposes mentioned above. Typical comments go like this: "This is my home, and they are trying to run my business." "My licensor is unreasonable."

"They always come at the worst times." "They disrupt my schedule." From our discussions, we identified many of the key problems with visits to family child care in-home businesses. In response to your questions and concerns, we have developed best practices and skills to make these visits more productive and worry-free for you.

Why Successful Visits Are Important

We cannot overemphasize how important your job is. You need to be able to concentrate on the care of the children in your program. But you must also attend to the requirements of running your business. You need the skills that help you connect with visitors in positive ways. These skills will enable you to get the support, guidance, and training you need to enhance your program.

Because of provider/visitor problems, subsidy programs are seeing reductions in enrollment. The Child and Adult Care Food Program (CACFP) is one of these programs; it is particularly important for feeding income-eligible children. Often the meals you serve are the only nutritious meals some children receive. When providers we spoke to were asked why they dropped out of subsidy programs, the most prevalent answer was this: you felt the visits were invasive, and you did not like the way the visitor enforced the regulations and requirements. This means a loss of income to you and a loss of important nutritional information, support, and resources for your clients. Clearly, the success of important programs like the CACFP depends a lot upon your having a good working relationship with the visitor.

Why Providers Need Support

Providers today are more independent and knowledgeable than in the past. You have access to many more high-quality training sessions. You can learn professionalism and how to operate your own individual child care business so that it gives you freedom and independence as your own boss. However, every business is governed by regulations and laws. Child care is regulated by many state, federal, health and safety, fire, and environmental statutes and ordinances that must be obeyed.

As a provider operating your own business, you might find yourself in conflict when your clients want you to overlook some regulations. For example, suppose your child care regulations state that a baby must be on the same floor level as you at all times. Yet you have a mother who wants you to put her baby down to sleep in an upstairs bedroom because she feels the baby will sleep longer in a quiet room. Your job as a licensed child care provider is to enforce and uphold all regulations, even if you believe the parent has a valid point. The tools in this manual will help you to interact with your clients in a positive manner while upholding the regulations.

Besides the regulatory aspects of visits, communications during a visit can be challenging. Visiting monitors coming into your home might not have good skills in this area. Some can be demanding and even aggressive in the way they carry out their duties. Others might be opinionated and want you to do things their way. When and how do you speak up? Where does their authority begin and end? Our goal is to assist you in developing skills that will lead you to interact with others productively and successfully so you can benefit the most from your visits.

How to Use This Manual

This manual is a reference guide. Each chapter discusses the skills you need so you can handle specific situations when someone is visiting your home.

Each chapter is designed to stand alone. This allows you to refer to the chapter that addresses a particular situation. Each chapter begins with a case study that presents a typical visit, complete with the stresses that can occur when providers are not adequately prepared or visitors are difficult. We present the challenges one by one, and we offer skill-based solutions. Later in each chapter, we offer a second case study that highlights the use of successful strategies. Chapters also include useful checklists to help you prepare for visits. The checklists are also available on Redleaf Press's website at www.redleafpress.org.

Mastering the skills in this manual requires practice, practice, practice. Keep the manual handy, and refer to it often.

LEAD YOUR FAMILY-TEAM

Starting on the right foot rarely takes on as much importance as when you decide to operate a family child care program. Your ability to respond effectively to the unexpected and to prepare for all the variables can make a very real difference in your degree of success.

CASE STUDY 1:
Susan's Family-Team Communication

Susan has invested a great deal of time and money in creating the child care setting of her dreams. She has long planned to open a business in her home; she hopes her business will allow her to be there for her husband and children while earning income doing what she loves best. Susan feels she has really done her homework on the best ways to organize her new business.

Susan has decorated and prepared her family room to accommodate small children. Even before enrolling them, she has purchased all the materials she could afford. When she applies for her license, she includes her own children's toys and equipment. She believes this will help to demonstrate her readiness to provide child care. Finally, when she has determined the appropriate amount of usable square footage, Susan includes her children's bedrooms as available child care space.

Susan is so sure that her family shares her enthusiasm for this project that she doesn't bother to ask her husband how he feels about having their family room transformed into a child care room. Nor does she think it necessary to talk with her children about other children playing in their rooms and using their personal toys and equipment. Feeling so excited herself, Susan just knows her family members will be thrilled to have her working at home and will simply ignore any minor inconveniences.

Once Susan receives her license, she decides that she will affiliate with a family child care system in her area. The system will help her become established and provide her with referrals, technical assistance, and enrollment in a food program. Susan begins caring for a few children in her neighborhood and schedules a visit with a representative from her local family child care system.

The night before the scheduled visit, Susan announces to her family that the following day is important because "they" are about to receive a visit that will help "their" business grow. Susan does not engage in a discussion with her family; rather, she simply tells them what is about to occur, assuming that everyone will be as excited as she is about this important step to success.

Much to her surprise, the visit does not go at all the way she has expected. The family child care system visitor finds numerous problems with Susan's setting. Several safety issues prevent Susan's environment from being an appropriate child care setting, including electrical outlet covers that have been removed and not replaced. The bathroom Susan has designated for child care has a broken safety latch on the cabinet, making medicines and other hazardous materials accessible to children. Much to Susan's embarrassment, when she is about to show the visitor her son's bedroom, they are greeted by a large sign on the door: DO NOT ENTER! PRIVATE PROPERTY!

The visitor explains to Susan that it is impossible to enroll her in the system until Susan demonstrates that all the safety and space issues are resolved. Susan feels blindsided. How has this happened?

CHALLENGE: Ensuring Cooperation from Family Members

Being a well-informed, enthusiastic business owner focused on success is unquestionably important to your role as a child care provider. It is equally important for anyone sharing your child care environment to be well informed and enthusiastic about the important job you are doing.

What has happened in Susan's case is rooted in poor communication with her family members. Although she understands her objectives in opening the child care business, she has not given her family the opportunity to express their opinions. Susan does not seem to understand that no one can more quickly sabotage the success of her family child care business than her own household's members. This is true not only of a provider just starting her business but also those of you who have long-established child care businesses.

SOLUTION: Create Collaboration

The process of collaborating with everyone in your household must begin with some serious thinking on your part. If you are just starting out, carefully examine all the aspects of providing child care before getting too excited about the idea. Although operating a home-based business does allow you to work from home, it does not necessarily provide you with more opportunity to be there for your family. Child care is a demanding profession. Talk with other providers who have experience balancing professional and family expectations. Do your best to understand and face the realities of home-based child care. Then, when you first approach your family about your business plan, be careful not to distort these realities just so the rest of your family will go along with the idea. Be truthful about the likely impact on your family members. Remember to include discussion about your family pets. Encourage all your household members, including children, to share their opinions. Be sure to actually listen when they offer feedback and suggestions!

Being willing to listen and compromise is especially important for veteran providers. As your own children grow, their needs change. Your nine-year-old who only a few years ago was a playmate for your child care attendees may now have very different priorities and a greater desire for privacy and personal space. It is important for you and your family to periodically revisit how everyone is feeling about and dealing with your home-based business. For example, in many states, you are required to operate within your quota during your business hours, and as a result, your own children may be unable to have their friends visit during child care hours. The irony of having a parent who is home and an environment that is geared toward children but cannot be fully used by your own children and their friends can be a bitter pill for them to swallow. Issues such as this require creative thinking and good teamwork between you and your family members.

SOLUTION: Be Specific about Your Expectations

You cannot assume that all your household members will understand or remember the licensing rules—or want to abide by them. You must be specific when explaining your expectations. For example, if the bathroom you are using for child care is the same bathroom shared by household members, everyone needs to understand the importance of keeping all hazards inaccessible to children. This same rule applies to other areas of your licensed space.

Similarly, if you expect that a household member will assist you in your business, make sure both of you understand what the role of helper entails. For instance, if you have a family pet and you have given your own child the responsibility of assuring that your outside play area is free of animal waste or other hazards, make sure your expectations are clearly stated and your son agrees to them. Do not assume agreement until he actually agrees to do what you require. You should also work out backup plans so that if the person assigned to a task cannot do it, you have another way to get the task done. Remember: the ultimate responsibility for a hazard-free environment always falls on you. A visitor to your child care setting will not accept that dangerous or unsanitary conditions in your home are somehow not your responsibility.

When allocating responsibilities, try to ensure that the individuals being assigned the tasks understand how this arrangement benefits them as well as you. Many providers assume their children and spouses are so happy to have them at home that everyone will pitch in to make the child care business a success. Be careful about such idealistic thinking. Sometimes the responses to your ideas and requests for help can be surprising . . . even disappointing. If you are asking your children and spouse to support your business, think about how they benefit from their contribution before you talk with them. Maintain a positive attitude and put yourself in their shoes as much as possible.

As your business grows and the needs of your family change, be as flexible as possible. Your daughter, who may have helped you in the past, may now have obligations at school that affect the time she is available to help you: increased homework, sports, and extracurricular activities may alter her hours and interests. You may find that after a certain length of time, your household members simply grow tired of sharing their living environment with your business. If this happens, you need to be proactive and responsive to the needs of your family members and keep them at the forefront during discussions. Each family has its own perspectives on finances, space, and available time. However, if you are willing to listen and make compromises, most issues can be resolved.

SOLUTION: Empower Your Own Children

Whenever possible, consider ways you can allow your children to maintain their own private spaces, toys, and materials they choose not to share with your child care. This is especially important for older children, who might return from school and find that their space and materials have been made available to young children. Imagine how displaced they might feel!

Sometimes it is easy to take the position that because you provide the roof over their heads and pay for the equipment and personal items in their rooms, your children should show their gratitude by sharing everything they own. However, you might want to take a moment to consider another perspective. Children who take pride in ownership are more likely to take special care of their personal space and equipment. Allowing your children some choice about what they share provides you and them with important teaching opportunities. Demonstrate through your behavior and your willingness to discuss solutions that you respect their personal space and that problem solving can be accomplished through respectful dialogue.

CHALLENGE: Maintaining "Visit Ready" Conditions

As Susan found out, it's not enough to "think" you are ready for a visit. You must know the requirements. Then you must be sure that your home always meets those requirements. The simple truth is that you need to operate under the assumption that on any given day you may receive an unannounced visit.

SOLUTION: Create and Use a Visit Ready Checklist

In business, one way operators ensure they are ready to receive clients or unexpected inspections is to use a daily checklist. If everything on a checklist is attended to, they feel assured that when they open their doors in the morning, they are ready for anyone who might visit.

Use the following checklist as a starting point and add what you need so each day is visit ready. The checklist can also be downloaded from www.redleafpress.org.

Your "Ready, Set, Go" List

CLEANLINESS AND SANITATION

___ Are rugs on which children crawl and play clean and hazard-free?

___ Are floors and counters free of debris and dirt?

___ Is the food preparation area sanitary?

___ Is children's food stored at appropriate temperatures?

___ Are the bathrooms clean and hazard-free?

___ Are washable toys and equipment regularly sanitized?

___ How does the child care environment smell?

___ Can you detect the scent of mold or mildew?

___ Are sleeping mats and bed linens appropriately clean and sanitary?

___ Are family pets accommodated in ways that are sanitary and odor-free?

___ _____

___ _____

___ _____

HEALTH AND SAFETY

___ Are all hazardous materials behind safety locks or at heights that make them inaccessible?

___ Do all electrical outlets have appropriate inserts or covers?

___ Are all exits free and clear of barriers or hazards, such as electrical cords?

___ Is all equipment, including bookcases, storage bins, TVs, and appliances, appropriately secured?

___ Is the napping area free of all hazards, such as curtain or blind cords?

___ Are all windows and screens secured appropriately?

___ Are safety gates secured and in place where required?

___ Are all required alarms (for example, smoke and carbon monoxide) in place and in working order?

___ Is there sufficient light?

___ Are all the room and water temperatures appropriate?

___ Are the materials used by children age appropriate, properly maintained, and regularly checked for broken or missing pieces and choking hazards?

___ Is the equipment used for children (for example, cribs, high chairs, car seats) regularly checked for safety or recall information?

___ Is the child care environment free of any environmental hazards, such as lead or secondhand smoke?

___ _____

___ _____

___ _____

PREP LIST FOR CHILDREN

___ Have you talked with the children about visitors to the child care setting—who they are and why they are here?

___ Have you set aside special items or created a "Visit Box" that children can use to occupy themselves during a visit?

___ Have you arranged your space to allow you to fully participate in a visit while still supervising the children in care?

___ Have the children practiced what to do when a visitor arrives?

___ _____

___ _____

___ _____

SOLUTION: Plan Good Storage Options from the Beginning

In keeping your environment consistently ready for visits, one of the most important aspects of good organization is appropriate storage. Rather than considering storage after you purchase equipment or materials, think about how you will store items before purchasing them.

It is a good idea to periodically walk into your child care setting and try to see it as if for the first time. Pretend you are the visitor. It is your job to evaluate the appropriateness of the child care environment. The individual materials and equipment may be great, but if there are too many things around, clutter can adversely affect your evaluation.

Remember that one of the primary elements of responsible early child care is providing room for children to grow. Think about your space in terms of how it helps your business grow. Think about ways you can effectively rotate your equipment and materials. Introduce activities that suit your space rather than overwhelm it. *Family Child Care Homes: Creative Spaces for Children to Learn* by Linda J. Armstrong can assist you with its creative ways to store equipment and materials so everything is not out and accessible at one time. You will find that recycling allows you to use materials longer and reduce your replacement costs.

CASE STUDY 2:
Susan Invites Everyone On Board

Susan loves children. Not only has she raised two of her own, but she has also provided care informally for neighborhood children for years. Now that her own two children are enrolled in school, Susan has decided that she wants to open a family child care program in her home. She feels that doing so will provide her with the opportunity to be compensated for work she really enjoys while being home when her husband and her children return from work and school.

Susan has done her homework. She has investigated how to become licensed and has attended an orientation training that provides clarification about the regulations and requirements for licensure. Susan has also read lots of books. She has chosen the curriculum she will use and has purchased materials that complement the activities and daily routines she wants to introduce. She has also investigated assessment tools and has selected one that corresponds perfectly with her curriculum.

Before doing any of this, however, Susan was smart enough to recognize that operating a child care business in her home would affect not only her but also her household members. She has made a point of talking with other licensed providers before initiating discussions with her family. She has asked questions and listened carefully while providers describe some of the challenges that can occur when blending a business with your home environment. Because Susan has invited this feedback, she is well prepared when she meets with her family to present her business plan.

Susan is enthusiastic about the benefits she sees in providing child care from the family's home, but she is also honest about the potential problems that might arise from this decision. She works very hard at helping her husband and children see that their opinions matter to her. She stresses that by working together, the family can resolve any issues that might arise.

Susan's business has been a great success. Her licensing visit is successful, as are subsequent business-related visits so far. Her family might not always be overjoyed at sharing their home with a group of small children, but no member of her family feels disempowered or unable to express an opinion. So far, her husband and children are willing participants in resolving any problems that arise.

Susan's preparation and thoughtful inclusion of her family before starting her business has been time well spent. Although things do not always go as expected, Susan has faced very few unpleasant surprises.

Checkpoints for Success

___ I have spoken with other experienced providers to help me better understand the challenges of combining my business and my home.

___ I have been proactive when approaching my household members and have engaged in honest discussions about the potential challenges of sharing living and business space.

___ I have done my homework and understand the regulations and requirements that govern the operation of my program. I have effectively communicated this information to my family members.

___ I have attempted to respect every household member's opinion, and I engage in effective problem-solving strategies to resolve any issues.

___ I have attempted not to assume anything when I am allocating business responsibilities to my household members. I have discussed each role and established appropriate ground rules.

___ I have implemented a checklist that assures me that my child care setting is always ready to receive clients, business-related visits, and inspections.

___ I have planned ahead and introduced appropriate storage and rotation of materials to optimize my available space.

THINK LIKE
A FAMILY MEMBER

Every family child care provider experiences conflicts with her own family. She will also have issues with the families of the children in her care. Like all problems, these can be solved by first clearly understanding the situation from the viewpoints of all involved and then taking proactive steps toward mutually agreeable solutions.

CASE STUDY 1:
Clara's Family Friction

Clara has been a family child care provider for about a year and a half. As Clara sits in the playroom watching the children pretend to be animals, she thinks about how much she enjoys interacting with them and how awed she remains by how their minds work. She reflects on the time since she opened her child care. She had been thrilled to care for children and to stay at home for her own three children. Though she is still excited about working with the children in her care, she has become frustrated and disappointed with her own family and the client families.

This morning's interactions with her family have become typical. Her fourteen-year-old daughter has left her makeup out on the counter in the bathroom used by the children. Her eight-year-old son is upset because the children got into his new dinosaur set and one of the dinosaurs is missing. Her two-year-old daughter has wanted to be held, and Clara feels guilty because she had to get ready for the child care children instead and could not give her the attention she wanted. Even her husband has made comments about the laundry piling up; he forgot to take the trash out when he left for work.

When the children started to arrive, one of the parents forgot to bring an extra change of clothes for her child, who is in the process of becoming toilet-trained. Clara has already sent this child home twice in her own daughter's clothes, which the parent has failed to return. Next, a grandparent dropped off her grandson, who was clutching a box of powdered sugar donut holes with one hand and stuffing some in his mouth with the other. When Clara mentioned her rule about not bringing sugary foods, the grandmother curtly stated, "He loves donuts, and my daughter pays you to watch him, not to tell us what he can eat." As Clara was starting to tell the grandmother why she has the rule, the phone rang. It was a parent she had interviewed, hoping to fill one of her empty slots. The parent told her that she had decided to take her child to another child care. This is the second potential client Clara has lost in the last two weeks.

Now, as Clara gets ready to sit on the floor to read the children a story about animals, she sighs and thinks that maybe she should close her child care and seek work outside her home. But when she looks at the children's eager faces, she knows she has a lot to give the children. She knows she needs advice about how to change things so her child care can succeed.

CHALLENGE: Managing Your Family's Involvement on an Ongoing Basis

It is normal for family members to feel resentful about the time you spend with other children and the changes that occur in their home to accommodate the child care children. Since Clara has not secured the ongoing support of her family, she experiences guilt and frustration. This keeps her from feeling joy and pride about developing a quality child care business.

SOLUTION: Focus on the Benefits for All

People start a child care businesses to be home for their own children, to eliminate the need to pay for child care, and to support their family's income. As a family child care provider and an independent business owner, you probably started with a wonderful vision of the child care you wanted to create. You put a lot of thought into your child care philosophy, environment, curriculum, daily schedule, developmentally appropriate materials, activities, safety, and children's nutrition. Like Clara, you felt pride and excitement from the beginning. Like Clara, you may also have become frustrated because your family does not consistently appreciate and support what you are doing.

One of the wonderful aspects of family child care is caring for children in a family atmosphere. You nurture and care for the children, and they take a lot of your time. Consider how your family may feel: after all, you are asking them to share their home, toys, beds, clothes, food . . . and you. What is the solution? Here are some positive actions you can take to improve the attitude and cooperation of your family.

1. Regularly identify the changes that occur in each family member's life that are directly related to your child care business. Consider

these things and think about how else your family members may be affected:

MATE

• Your time and priorities might change according to your child care schedule. Mealtimes might be delayed until the last child is picked up; you might still be caring for children during dinner. Your mate comes home after a long day; it has been a long day for you, too, and it is not over. You might not have started dinner, and your kitchen and living area might be filled with baby furniture, toys, and children. Your mate might resent how much your child care business affects your availability for the family.

• New responsibilities arise—for example, your property might need to be cleaned and maintained differently; hazards, including old paint cans, oil, and antifreeze must be removed; broken fences and steps might need to be fixed or replaced; walkways must be clean of snow and ice so families and other visitors don't fall when arriving at your home. Your mate now has new, unexpected responsibilities.

• Your mate might start to realize that liability issues can arise when you run a business out of your home. New concerns might arise that have not been discussed. For example, you might need to make changes in your home by installing a gate around your fireplace and at the top of stairs, radiator covers, a fence around a swimming pool, or storage areas for child care supplies.

• Your mate might need to take on more chores because you are working long hours during the day, and the household chores themselves have changed.

CHILDREN

- During child care hours, you are working and cannot always take care of your own children's needs immediately. Your children might be struggling to share you with the other children. You might also feel guilty when you ask your own children to be patient while you care for another child.
- Because the children in care might use any of your children's toys and possessions that are left around, your older children must learn to put away anything they want to keep out of the child care children's hands.
- Your children might not be able to invite their friends over after school when your program is fully enrolled.
- Your children might resent having to always make sure they close gates and keep stairs free from clutter.
- They might miss out on fun things when you are unable to take them to games, practices, and friends' houses after school.

2. After you have identified the changes operating a family child care business might impose, think about any mutual goals and benefits it might offer each family member. Identify how these benefits can outweigh the disadvantages. For example:

MATE

- You will be adding to the family income. This might be a necessity, and when you and your mate look at the cost of care for your own children, the family child care business could be the desired solution.

CHILDREN

- Teenagers should understand what it means to them personally for the family's income to increase. It might help to pay for guitar lessons, sports equipment, a special family vacation, or simply handling household expenses with less stress.
- School-age children should understand the advantage of being able to come home after school.
- Very young children cannot understand needing to share you with other children. However, you can feel comfortable knowing that you can be there for your children during the day. You also know that the social skills they are learning by spending time with other young children, like taking turns, are important for their development.

3. Plan regular family meetings. Schedule them once a month or once a week to fit the needs of your family.

PLAN YOUR MEETINGS

- Before each meeting, think carefully about what your goal is for the discussion and share it with your family. If your goal is to have more help and cooperation in the mornings, make sure that you stick to this topic. If you need to ease the feelings of one or more family members, remember to listen and focus on the root of the problem.
- Prepare for the discussion by thinking of possible solutions you can propose, and invite family members to come up with their own possible solutions. For example, if your eight-year-old son is upset because his toys are being broken, you might offer to get him a storage box that locks. Encourage him to decorate his box with stickers.

Give him one key and keep the other. Encourage your son to put anything special into the box so it will be safe.

4. Keep your family aware of progress toward family goals.

FAMILY UPDATES

- Record the progress toward the goal and put it where everyone in the family can see it. For example, if your family's goal is to take a special vacation, keep a chart measuring money saved for the trip.
- Whenever possible, praise your family members' accomplishments on behalf of the child care business and let them know that their contributions are appreciated.

CHALLENGE: Keeping Clients Happy While Meeting Your Own Goals

Parents, grandparents, and legal guardians are your clients. When you are caring for their children, conflicts can arise. Clients may feel that because they pay you, they can set the rules, like the grandparent who dropped off the child with a box of powdered sugar donuts. Conflicts can arise in many areas: payments, discipline, toilet training, TV watching, paperwork, late pickup and drop-off, and meals.

SOLUTION: Put Your Philosophy and Corresponding Needs in Writing

The steps that follow are designed to help you determine your program's policies and make them clear to your clients. Good planning and communication help your program be more successful. Sometimes you need to be even more assertive; please read chapter 5 for additional skills to use when dealing with clients who are being difficult.

The more you can communicate your philosophy of your child care, the easier you can determine whether a child will be a good fit for you. Your contract should reflect how you run your business and what you expect of parents. Always take the time to listen to prospective clients.

STEP 1: PHILOSOPHY

Begin by defining your child care philosophy. You need to be clear about your program's goals. Your philosophy is reflected in your curriculum, and it comes through when you express your opinions about how children learn. For help in defining your philosophy, use the "Philosophy Worksheet" that follows. It can also be found on the Redleaf Press website at www.redleafpress.org.

Your philosophy of child care is really about you. Usually it is based on your strengths and reflects your experiences with children. For example, if you enjoy being outdoors and believe that exposure to fresh air and a science-in-nature approach are the best ways for young children to learn, your program should reflect this.

Sample philosophy statement: I believe that art and music are very important to the development of young children. Children should have the freedom to explore music and art in a loosely structured setting. Therefore, I will schedule a portion of each day to explore art or music. My child care will include a table to explore art and a wide space in which to move to music. I will nurture and guide the children to express themselves during the art and music time.

Philosophy Worksheet

By answering these questions, you can determine how you want your child care to operate and how you want to set up your environment. After you examine the answers to your questions, you should be able to write a philosophy statement that accurately describes your business.

1. What are your special interests, and how can they be applied to your family child care curriculum?

_____

_____

_____

_____

2. Are you more comfortable with structure or with lots of flexibility in your day?

_____

_____

_____

_____

3. How do you use your available space? Does a large part of your daily routine take place in a single child care room, or do you use most of the space in your home?

_____

_____

_____

4. Do you see yourself primarily as a nurturer or as a teacher?

_____

_____

_____

MY PHILOSOPHY STATEMENT

_____

_____

_____

STEP 2: CONTRACT

Prepare your contract for families. Your philosophy directly influences the items in your contract. For example, your curriculum might consist of activities to help children meet developmental goals that include being able to dress independently for going outdoors. Therefore, your contract should state that families must bring appropriate clothing for outdoor play. Because outdoor play is so much a part of your curriculum, it is vital that your clients comply with your request.

In addition, your contract should reflect your philosophy on children bringing toys from home, including toy weapons, action figures, videos, and other items that might lead to conflicts or overly aggressive play. Your philosophy on nutritional standards, discipline, naptime, and toilet training should all be clear in your mind and corresponding expectations and rules spelled out in your contract.

STEP 3: TALK TO THE RESPONSIBLE ADULTS

Discuss your contract and your philosophy with prospective clients and make sure they understand your reasons for your rules. Discussing these upfront helps families determine if your program is a good fit for their children. If you make any changes to your contract, take time to explain them to already enrolled families.

If Clara had discussed her policy about bringing food to child care and explained that her curriculum included social developmental goals during meals, the family would have clearly understood that those sugary donuts were not appropriate. Rather than arguing with the grandparent, Clara could have referred the clients to her contract and explained to them that they needed to tell the grandparent that donuts are not acceptable.

CHALLENGE: Recruiting New Clients

In many areas, family child care can be very competitive. Especially if you are just starting out, you may need a while to build up your reputation. In this case study, even though Clara was getting interviews with families, they were deciding to take their children elsewhere. She was not sure what was going wrong with her interviews. This section examines the interview process from the perspective of a family seeking child care. Understanding the family's perspective helps you make the child's adjustments to care easier on everyone, especially the children, since children adjust to child care better when there is continuity in the way things are done. It also helps the family feel comfortable and opens the lines of communication that are so necessary when you are caring for another person's child.

SOLUTION: Present Your Program as a Professional

When families seeking child care meet you for the first time, they use all their senses to evaluate you and your program. Each one of the senses detects information that can affect your ability to recruit new clients. What we see, hear, and smell form our first and sometimes most lasting impressions. Prospective parents are looking for a capable and caring individual to care for their child.

First take a look at yourself. Think carefully about the first impression you make. Parents are looking for a safe, nurturing, and interesting environment for their child. The senses really are important and tell a prospective client a lot about your environment.

THE SENSE OF SMELL

Coming into your child care home from outside, what do you smell? A family child care environment should smell like the good things that are happening there: healthy foods, flowers and greenery, children's paints, crayons, and clay. How your environment smells sends a powerful message to children and families. The following are things to be aware of as you evaluate the smells in your home.

Pets

Many providers include pets as part of their child care curriculum. Some providers allow their own household pets to be in the same areas of the home that are used for child care. Because you live with these pets, you might have lost the ability to smell odors that have been present for a long time. Ask your licensor or a trusted friend to evaluate any animal odors in your home. Keep in mind that fish tanks, bird cages, and containers housing gerbils or hamsters can be sources of odors. Don't forget litter boxes. If you can smell the litter box, whether or not it is an area of the house the children use, it is a problem that must be corrected.

Diaper and Toilet Odors

If visitors smell urine and/or feces odors in your home, the first question they will ask is, "Where and how frequently does this provider dispose of diapers?" If you can detect these odors, search for the source. Is the smell coming from trash that has not been covered or disposed of? Is the odor coming from children whose diapers you are not changing often enough? Make sure you have a procedure to dispose of dirty diapers in a closed container that is emptied and sanitized often.

Garbage

Don't allow your trash containers to become so full that they are overflowing. Empty them often and be aware of any odors that may be coming from the trash. Wash and sanitize containers often. Trash that is overflowing onto the floor or is kept in an uncovered container can be a hazard.

Mold and Mildew

Many providers use the basement to separate their child care space from the rest of the house. If children are cared for in your basement, make sure the area is well ventilated and well lit. Consider running a dehumidifier that is set to automatically remove excess moisture from the air. Mold and mildew can cause illness and allergic reactions in children.

Disinfectants and Harsh Cleansers

Many disinfectants and cleansers contain harmful chemicals such as ammonia, petrochemicals, and volatile organic compounds (VOCs). Over a period of time, chlorine bleach, too, can be damaging to a child's health. If you can smell chlorine bleach, there is probably residue on surfaces or in the air. Check the amount and mixture of bleach solution you are using, and after allowing the solution to air-dry for the solution's designated dwell time, rinse the area with water and dry with a clean cloth.

Cigarette Smoke

Cigarette smoke has a powerful smell that permeates everything. If you or family members smoke, you need to pay particular attention to where the smoking takes place. Secondhand smoke is hazardous to the health of children, as is thirdhand smoke. The smoke lingers after the tobacco product is no longer present. If you or your child care environment smells of smoke, it may be the number one reason why you are not enrolling children.

THE SENSE OF HEARING

When prospective clients come into your child care environment, they are very aware of the sound level. There is a difference between noise and sound. We do not expect a child care environment to be quiet, but there is a difference between the sound of young children squealing with joy while playing a game and the noise of a child screaming to be heard. Sound is often thought of as something pleasant to hear, whereas noise is usually negative and unpleasant. A visitor should hear the happy, busy hum of children who are involved in activities they enjoy. Here are some factors you should evaluate.

Indoor Volume

If you need to raise your voice to be heard, determine why. Think about what a visitor is hearing. Is the sound coming from the TV? Is the volume loud? Are the children watching the TV, or is it on all day as background noise? Families might assume that you use the TV to keep the children busy. If you have a schedule and a developmental curriculum each day, it should not be necessary for the TV to be on. It only serves as a distraction.

Does a prospective client hear the busy hum of children's voices, or are the children out of control? We know that many times when a visitor comes, the children can become disruptive and the environment can become chaotic. It is important to plan ahead for appointments with prospective clients. Either have an assistant ready to do an activity with the children, or prepare the children for visitors and give them an activity. Some providers have a special "Visitor Box" filled with craft supplies that only come out when someone visits the home.

Prospective families also listen to the way children talk to one another and the way you address the children. Is the tone positive, or do the children speak to each other in demeaning ways? Are the children mimicking your words, tone, and body language? Do you speak in a different tone of voice to the visitors than you do to the children? Do you make demeaning comments about an unruly child to prospective clients in front of the child? Your visitors are going to be watching you closely. They observe changes in your tone of voice or mannerisms that differ when you talk to them and when you address the children. For example, consider this scenario: a provider is talking to a parent, and a small child comes over and leans on the provider's knee. Does the provider acknowledge the child's presence by putting her hand on the child, or does the provider move her leg, turn away from the child, and say, "Go play"?

Household Members

If you have household members present during your interview, pay attention to how you interact with them too. For example, if your own child is present, do you treat your child differently than the child care children? Is your child demanding or intimidating toward the other children? Often it is the provider's own children who are disruptive during an interview. They might say to the visitor, "I am not one of the child care children." How you deal with this situation leaves an impression on the prospective client. Plan ahead so you can address the situation in a professional manner.

Absence of Sound

If a visitor comes into your child care and the environment is very quiet, unless it is naptime, the person may conclude that you run a very rigid and overly structured program. Even when the sounds in your child care may be loud, make sure they are productive, happy sounds.

THE SENSE OF SIGHT

Start your evaluation from the outdoor area of your home. What do you see? Is the entrance to your home free from clutter? Do you have a fence? Is it in good condition? What about the child care outdoor play area? Make sure it is clean and safe for the children. Prospective clients' impressions begin before they even enter your home. First impressions and assumptions about your business practices can be made from what they see upon arriving at your home. After evaluating the outdoor area, enter your child care as if for the first time. Be honest with yourself, and do not be influenced by what you expect to see. Really examine what you see. Here are some things you should evaluate.

Yourself

Take a look at how you are dressed. Is your attire clean and appropriate for working with children? Is your hair neat? Are you calm and professional in the way you greet your prospective clients? If you present yourself looking frazzled and disheveled, you do not instill confidence in families that you have the ability to care for their children.

Clutter

Your child care environment should offer ample room for children and adults to move about freely. Is that what you see, or do the areas appear crowded and cluttered? Some clutter is normal in a child care environment, but it should not pose a hazard or risk, and it should not be so extensive that children cannot productively engage in activities. Look around: Do you see broken toys, too many materials, and too little storage?

Spaces That Support Social Interactions

Does a visitor see spaces that encourage social interaction? Are there spaces where a child can sit quietly and play or look at a book? Here is a desirable scenario if you use your living room and kitchen for your child care space: the kitchen table offers booster seats and high chairs arranged so that the children can socialize when eating and doing activities. The living room contains a comfortable corner with pillows where a child can enjoy some quiet time. Toys, puzzles, books, and blocks are kept in storage bins that are accessible to the children. The children's artwork is arranged on a bulletin board in your kitchen. Your environment looks like a home, but it also looks like an inviting area for children.

THE SENSE OF TOUCH

Prospective clients may not touch a lot of surfaces in your home, but it is important that they see that you have put thought into the areas where their child will be. Babies especially learn about their world through touch. Is there carpeting on the floor? Is it warm and clean for a baby to sit and crawl on? Is the furniture torn or ripped, or is it soft and inviting to sit on? Are there sticky surfaces in your home? Think about where you are going to sit when prospective clients visit, and make sure that the area is clean and free of food residue and animal hair. Nothing turns a parent off more than a sticky environment.

PUTTING IT ALL TOGETHER

When prospective clients enter your home, do they get an overall positive feeling or impression? Stand still, look around, listen, take a deep breath, and see what your own first impression is of your environment.

When developing the overall impression you want people to have of your child care, also think about your marketing materials. Consider this story from Donna, one of the authors of this book.

> A provider in my child care system was complaining that she was not getting any referrals for children. We had been referring her to prospective clients and wondered why she was not even getting visits. One afternoon, I called her and got her voice mail. Her message went like this: for ten seconds, I heard a baby crying very loudly, then the provider's voice yelling over the crying baby, saying, "Obviously I can't come to the phone right now! Leave a message."
>
> When I questioned her about her message, she laughed and said it was a joke. I explained to her that prospective clients didn't know her, and her message was giving the wrong impression. No wonder parents weren't leaving a message!

Do you have printouts of policies, procedures, and rules for your child care? Some providers have found that giving potential clients a folder is very helpful, especially in ensuring that they do not miss anything important during their discussion with the family. Make sure your paperwork is clean and professional. You don't want to hand a parent a wrinkled and soiled contract to sign or present paperwork that includes typos or other errors. You might include photographs of happy children from your program playing, taking field trips, or enjoying parties.

Learning how to view your child care through the eyes of your clients helps you to foresee and resolve problems before they arise.

CASE STUDY 2:
Clara Addresses Problems through the Families' Perspectives

A few weeks ago, Clara had a visit from her licensor. The licensor was very happy with what she observed of Clara's program. Clara shared her frustration with her family members and some of her clients with the licensor. She was thrilled when the licensor offered to help.

Since then, Clara has taken the licensor's suggestion and has looked at her child care through her family's eyes. From a different perspective, she has to admit that her business has had an impact on each family member's life. She also acknowledges that she never considered discussing these changes with her family.

Clara's next thought has been about the benefits for her family. She knows she is taking some of the burden off her husband by helping with the family finances. She also feels pleased that field hockey equipment for her daughter has been purchased with money earned from her business. Clara knows her son loves coming directly home after school. She feels satisfied that she can be there each day for him. Even her little one, who was quite demanding before Clara opened her child care business, is learning to take turns. Clara feels very confident that the benefits outweigh the inconveniences.

Clara has started to hold family meetings when any problems come up. She prepares well before each meeting, and the positive outcomes are evident. Just this morning, her fourteen-year-old made a point of picking up all her things from the bathroom without being reminded. Her son carefully put his "treasures" in his box and slid it under the bed before he left for school. Her husband remembered to take out the trash and even offered to fix a broken handle on the cabinet before he went to work. Not every day goes this smoothly, but at least they are all trying to cooperate. Even Clara has made concessions by cutting back her hours of care by one hour and deciding not to serve dinner anymore, so dinnertime can be just for the family.

Clara is also evaluating her communication with her clients. She has prepared a flyer for the clients, outlining her philosophy and stating her policies for toilet training, meals, and developmental goals for the children and her child care. All of the families are happy to hear about the learning that is happening during the children's daily routines.

Clara and the licensor have looked at the child care from a prospective client's viewpoint. Using their senses, they evaluated the environment. Clara was surprised to learn that her house smelled like garbage because the trash can lid was broken so that it could not be closed tightly. She also admitted that sometimes the can did not get emptied until it was overflowing. These were easy things to fix.

Examining her paperwork for prospective clients, she has discovered that she is a little disorganized and often has to search for enrollment forms, contracts, and other vital papers. She knows she must present herself in a more professional manner. She has changed the voice message on her phone from her teenager daughter singing and giggling to a professional business request to leave a message. She has organized her paperwork and feels prepared for future appointments with prospective clients.

Checkpoints for Success

Putting yourself in another's shoes and looking at your business from a different perspective gives you insight into what others might be thinking. Often, because we are so close to a situation, we find it hard to understand the behavior or viewpoint of others. Asking for help when you need it, and recognizing and validating others' perspectives will allow you to feel more satisfaction and fulfillment in operating your business. Use the following checklist to help you identify your strengths and weaknesses. Doing so gives you an opportunity to think about any positive changes you might make.

____ I identify the changes my business continues to make on my family members' lives.

____ I identify the benefits my business has for each family member.

____ I plan and hold regular family discussions.

____ I periodically ask a trusted colleague or friend to evaluate the first impressions my child care business makes by using all her senses.

____ I identify ways to professionally communicate my philosophy, policies, and goals to clients.

BE PREPARED FOR VISITS

Making a good first impression is critical when you are interviewing prospective clients. A good first impression is also important when you receive visitors whose role includes evaluating the service you provide.

One of the ways to ensure a good first impression is to master all the rules and regulations you are obliged to comply with. Once you understand your obligations, you can better prepare for the many expected and unexpected situations that can occur.

CASE STUDY 1:
Maria—Unprepared for the Unexpected

Maria is a newly licensed family child care provider and has been working very hard for about six months to establish her business. Today is Friday, and Maria is having a bad day. She is feeling like the only good thing about today is that it's the final day of a frustrating week. All the children in Maria's program have had head colds. Their illnesses are not serious enough to warrant staying at home, at least according to their families, but the colds are serious enough to have spread throughout Maria's enrollment.

In addition, Maria recently accepted a new child into her program, and this is the third day in a row the child has attended without the parent remembering to bring the child's required paperwork. Maria is unclear how much time she has before this creates a regulatory problem. She feels uncomfortable because if the child becomes sick or has an accident, Maria has no medical information or signed permission forms to authorize medical assistance. She is reluctant to appear angry or too pushy with a client; however, the unresponsiveness of this parent has certainly added to Maria's stress.

To add even more stress to an already overwhelming week, Maria's own school-age child, Angela, is home sick with the same cold that has spread throughout Maria's enrollment. To be perfectly honest, Maria is not feeling all that well herself. She is concerned because she is not quite sure whether Angela's presence during child care hours throws off the required adult/child ratio reflected in her family child care license.

Maria's day is about to get worse. She has just looked out her window to see her licensor getting out of her car and heading up the driveway. Maria cannot believe her bad luck. Why is this happening? Maria attempts to remember whether or not her licensor has the authority to just drop by without calling ahead to schedule an appointment. Her mind starts going in ten different directions: *Why is she coming after only six months? Is there some type of problem? Did someone complain? What is the required time frame for having all the children's paperwork, and why can't I remember the rule about my own child being at home during child care hours?*

By the time Maria opens her front door, she is not only panicked, she is also preparing herself for what she is sure will be a negative interaction. As a result, Maria is growing more and more defensive by the minute.

CHALLENGE: Dealing with Unforeseen Variables

Does anything about this case study sound familiar? It's difficult to imagine anyone providing family child care for any length of time without experiencing at least one of the problems Maria is facing. In business, as in life, unexpected circumstances always arise. In child care business, this is especially true: you are constantly placed in situations in which you need to deal with various personalities and issues. When you include all the possible circumstances that might involve your own household members, it is no wonder that sometimes things can feel overwhelming. How can you realistically prepare yourself for all the variables that may occur during the operation of your business?

SOLUTION: Stay Current with Regulations

One of the best ways you can prepare is by operating your program in a manner that is proactive rather than reactive. Legal, regulatory, and contractual requirements differ from state to state and agency to agency. You might live in a state where a license is required to provide child care in your home, or you could live in a state where you simply need to register in order to provide care. Your state might have a centralized licensing authority or various county agencies. Regardless of where the requirements originate or whether you agree with all of them, it is extremely important that you know what they are. Think of it this way: if you're driving your car and you are stopped because you have disregarded a traffic regulation, responding that you were "unaware of the law" does not excuse you from your responsibility to comply. The same holds true in your child care business.

You must understand any regulations or legal requirements you have agreed to comply with. Always keep a copy of your regulations at hand while you are operating your program. If the regulations change, make sure you update your copy. Refer to them when you have questions. Be careful not to place yourself at a disadvantage by seeking advice about regulatory information from other providers, because they may or may not know all the regulations. Having regulations on hand and referring to them frequently helps you feel less vulnerable if you do receive an unannounced visit.

Additional helpful hints include the following.

- If you still have questions after reviewing your regulations, don't procrastinate—ask! Contact your licensing authority to get the correct answers. Don't wait and find yourself in Maria's situation.

- Regulatory language can sometimes be confusing. For example, some regulations can appear to be open to interpretation. Don't be shy about asking the same question repeatedly until you are sure that you fully understand the answer.

- Think about scenarios that could occur, and ask questions about how regulations would apply in those circumstances. For example, Maria needs to know how having her own school-age child home during child care hours affects her adult-child ratio.

- Don't be afraid to ask questions about mandatory monitoring visits— their expected frequency, whether they will be announced or unannounced. Request information in advance about the procedure for challenging possible citations that might occur as the result of a visit.

- Ask about variance opportunities that allow you to meet the intent of a regulation in a somewhat different manner from what is stated. For example, can you use a local park within walking distance of your home if you do not have an adjacent yard suitable as an outside play area?

- Keep a written list of questions that may come up during operation of your program. You can refer to this list during a visit, or you can

contact the responsible authority to get answers to your questions
when you need them.

- If your state regulations are changing, make sure you find out specifically what the changes involve, how those changes impact your child
care program, and when the changes will occur.

- Find out what options are available for feedback, and make an attempt
to participate in your state's procedures for creating or changing
existing child care regulations. Most states are required to hold public
hearings so that affected parties can express their opinions before
regulations go into effect. Your participation is important.

If Maria had remained up to date on her regulations, she might feel more
confident and less defensive when she opens her door. If she knew the policy
for conducting unannounced visits in her state, for example, she would realize that her licensor is required to conduct an unannounced visit within six
months and that because of this, she is actually overdue for a visit. In other
words, knowing her own business could have greatly reduced Maria's appre-
hension about the timing and reason for the visit. Knowledge is power. Providers who feel empowered are better able to interact with other professionals
in a positive manner.

CHALLENGE: Understanding Your Role during Visits

It's no secret that child care providers have busy, labor-intensive jobs. After
the children have returned to their homes at the end of the day, you are not
necessarily looking for more business-related visitors to invite in. But licensors are not the only individuals who conduct professional or business-related
visits to your home, and you should take the time to understand the role and
responsibilities of all the individuals required to visit your child care setting.

Individuals required to conduct visits may include, but are not limited to,

- building inspectors
- health and safety inspectors
- food program monitors
- family child care system monitors
- mentors
- accreditation specialists
- social workers
- early intervention specialists
- Head Start professionals
- Resource and Referral representatives
- clients

SOLUTION: Understand the Goal of Each Type of Visit

You become empowered when you fully understand the role of the person visiting your home. For example, make sure you understand the difference between a recommendation and a requirement. This is important because it is very probable that the various professionals who conduct visits in your home will share all types of information with you. You need to distinguish between what is simply someone else's opinion and something you are required to do by regulation or law. The following list contains useful tips about the various visits that may be conducted in your home.

HEALTH AND SAFETY INSPECTIONS

If the requirements in your state include an inspection from your local building, fire, or health departments, do yourself a favor and find out exactly the scope of their inspection before the visit takes place. It is a lot easier to be proactive and prepare for an inspection if you know ahead of time what to expect. Don't wait and then be forced to rely solely on the person conducting the inspection to dictate its scope. For example, if you have an addition to your home to accommodate child care, will the building inspection be limited to the addition, or will it include your entire house?

Make sure you understand exactly what is required of you, and don't be afraid to call and ask questions before the visit takes place. If you feel an inspector has overreached his authority, you are in a better position to call attention to this when you are well prepared. When you are knowledgeable about specific requirements as well as your rights, you are less likely to feel intimidated.

MONITORING VISITS

Many agencies other than licensing authorities might conduct monitoring visits in your home: voucher agencies, food programs, family child care systems, social service agencies, and Resource and Referral agencies, to name just a few. These visits usually occur as a result of a contractual agreement. The most important protection you have is knowledge of what is contained in your contract. What are the expectations placed on you, and what expectations should you have regarding the contracting agency? Know what you are signing before you sign it. Do not simply rely on an agency representative to explain to you what is contained in your contract. Carefully read it, and make sure any questions you have are answered before you sign anything. Never sign a contract that is written in a language you cannot understand.

Once you understand your agreement, you can seek assistance in creating procedures to help you comply with what you have agreed to do. For example, if your food program stipulates that you need to be filling out menus at the same time you are serving lunch (this is known as "point of service"), you need to be prepared to do exactly that. One of the easiest ways to create unnecessary stress, as well as confrontational visits, is to ignore what you have agreed to do and hope you will not be visited. It simply doesn't work that way.

MENTORING AND OBSERVATIONS

Usually, when a mentor or an observer visits your home, the visit has been scheduled. Often this type of visit is at your request and may be connected to referrals or accreditation. There are exceptions to this, however. In some states, regulatory authorities use mentors or consultants to assist providers in correcting problems that the authority has identified as noncompliant. In some instances, providers are required to pay for these services as part of their corrective action plan. In some instances, family child care systems assign a mentor to a provider in the hope that positive peer support will help improve her program. In situations like these, a provider might not have a choice of the person who conducts the visits.

Remember that mentoring visits—even the ones that occur at your own request—are not intended to be personal, whether or not you are familiar with your visitor. They should be considered business-related visits. Keep in mind that although the individual conducting the visit is usually there to provide you with assistance, she also has an ethical and, in some cases, a legal responsibility to the children in your program. Protect yourself and your program by understanding that your obligation to ensure each child's well-being never changes because of your relationship with the person conducting the visit.

PROSPECTIVE CLIENT VISITS

Prepare for prospective client interviews by taking time to consider what your priorities would be if you were visiting a child care setting for the purpose of enrolling your own child. What are some of the things you would like to see and hear so you felt comfortable about enrollment? Make a list of your priorities, and compare that list with what routinely happens in your child care program.

Providers who feel confident about the quality of their care usually operate the best programs. When you feel confident, you are better able to demonstrate to prospective clients during interviews and visits why your program is special and why it meets the needs of each child enrolled. Clients use all their senses when evaluating the care environment for their child, so make sure that your program leaves a good first impression. Establish good provider-client communication by developing an effective provider-client contract. (See chapter 2 for information on the personal thinking you should do before preparing a contract.)

As part of your proactive approach, review your existing contract and investigate a variety of contracts that work well in family child care. *Family Child Care Contracts & Policies*, 3rd edition, by Tom Copeland is a good book that deals with this topic. You can also request suggestions from other providers, mentors, or other professionals. Well-written contracts use understandable language to help reduce stressful situations. Make sure your contract provides a clear outline of what a client can expect from you and what you expect from your client. Describe how information is to be shared to minimize surprises and help you and your client avoid confrontational visits.

A good contract communicates the various regulations that govern how you operate your program. For example, regulations stating how many children you can provide care for at any one time or the necessity for required paperwork are important for the families of children in your care to understand and comply with. "Sick policies" in your contractual information help clarify your expectations. Think how helpful having this would have been for Maria in the case study! If Maria had clearly stated her requirements for enrollment and the consequences of not meeting those requirements, she might not have had to chase after parents for required paperwork.

CHALLENGE: Effectively Anticipating a Visit

Whether a visit is scheduled or unexpected, consistent attention to your program allows you to effectively anticipate any type of visit that might occur. To anticipate a visit effectively, you should have done everything in your power to assure that your environment and your program are appropriate and comply with relevant regulations and laws. You should have been proactive and taken all the necessary steps to feel empowered and able to interact as a professional without feeling afraid or intimidated. When you have taken these needed steps, you can feel confident when you open your front door. The following are some of the steps you can take to maintain your positive focus and prepare for the various types of business-related visits that occur.

SOLUTION: Remain Informed and Up to Date

An invaluable way to reduce stress and build confidence is to stay up to date with the information on quality early child care. Whether you are involved in child care for the short term or the long haul, you enhance your program by staying well informed. Taking courses, reading books, and attending trainings are great ways to obtain reliable information. As new information becomes available on how children develop and grow, your program should reflect the best practices arising from such information. We now know, for example, that infants benefit greatly from consistent and nurturing verbal and physical interaction. Your curriculum should reflect this. Include the developmental goals of infants as well as those of toddlers and preschoolers.

It's a lot easier to maintain your composure and self-assurance during a visit when you know you are doing all you can to operate your child care program proactively. Many states now require a specific number of training hours before you can renew a license or registration. Look at this regulation as an opportunity for professional development, a way to stay informed, and a chance to enhance your child care résumé. Incorporating curriculum that works well with your current enrollment and understanding the developmental needs of all the children in your care can help you focus your attention and effectively anticipate visits. Rather than feeling uncomfortable because you fear a visit will demonstrate what is wrong with your program, you can feel confident that you can demonstrate all the things you are doing right.

SOLUTION: Care about Yourself

Often, when people work out of their homes, they are tempted to take a very informal approach to their personal presentation. Parents who complain about their child care provider sometimes say that the provider was in what appeared to be her pajamas when a child was dropped off and was still wearing the same attire when the child was picked up at the end of the day.

Although you are working from your home, remember that you are a professional providing a very important service. Your physical appearance, your energy level, and your demeanor all affect how your child care program is viewed. You are the driving force behind your business. If you are answering your front door looking disheveled and overwhelmed, you are setting the tone for a visit that might be uncomfortable for everyone involved. We all have bad days now and then, but it is a mistake to assume that parents or professionals visiting your program cannot tell the difference between a bad day and a poorly run child care business.

Everyone feels better and more confident when rested, clean, and looking one's best. Not only does practicing healthy personal habits allow you a better opportunity to model appropriate behavior for the children in your care, but it also allows you to feel confident and professional when dealing with adults visiting your program. Some providers have developed a type of uniform they wear while caring for children so they look professional and keep their own clothes clean. It might be a smock that protects your clothing and can be changed quickly if it becomes stained or dirty.

Child care can be exhausting, so take good care of yourself. Make sure you are getting sufficient rest. You must actively participate in your program, and good participation requires positive energy. Think about your profession and the types of activities you are involved in during each day. Wear clothes that are comfortable and practical, but do not forget that you are a professional. Visits are generally much less stressful if you feel comfortable with your appearance.

SOLUTION: Get Organized

Take a moment to think about what your impression would be if you visited your doctor's office and the secretary started searching under the desk or behind the cabinets for your file. You would probably not feel a great deal of confidence in the professional service you have come to receive. You have a right to expect a commercial business to be better organized. The same holds true for your business! You, too, are offering a professional service of great value and importance to your clients.

When you are organized and proactive, you do a great deal to minimize the stress of an unanticipated visit. Required paperwork is often an area in which providers feel they have been unfairly evaluated. As part of your proactive approach to visits, realize that an important aspect of most monitoring visits involves reviewing your child care records. Why not have all your paperwork organized, up to date, and easily accessible? The classic line "I know I had that file, but . . . " does nothing to improve the dynamic of a visit. A few providers choose to deflect their responsibility by blaming their clients: "It's not my fault that I don't have signed permission, because the parent never gave it to me." Your clients need to be informed that your program is subject to unannounced visits. Don't be afraid to tell families that their children cannot attend until you have received all of their required paperwork.

The following are things to consider as you get your paperwork organized.

FILE CABINET

If you do not currently have a file cabinet, think about investing in one. A well-organized file cabinet can save you a great amount of time and grief. Remember that the information contained in your child care records is usually viewed as confidential. These files should not be left on the kitchen table. A file cabinet allows you to keep files in a protected, organized manner. It also encourages you to store all your records in one location so you have easy access when files need to be reviewed by appropriate professionals.

ORGANIZATIONAL SYSTEM

Most states require that you maintain child care records for children who have left your program for a designated period. In organizing your storage area, make sure you can identify and separate those files from those of currently enrolled clients. Think about creating separate folders for items such as your attendance records and menus. Try color coding your files for easy identification (for example, blue for menus, green for attendance). If you are required to keep attendance schedules on file for your employees or assistants, make sure that information is organized and filed separately. You should have a separate file for each child and each employee.

UPDATES

You need to set aside sufficient time to address your required paperwork. Some providers say they chose the child care profession because they wanted to avoid the responsibility of paperwork. The truth is that maintaining well-organized and accurate records is an important and inescapable part of your role as a family child care provider. If you set aside a small amount of time each day, keeping your records current does not seem like such an overwhelming task. This is especially true of your attendance records. Double check to make sure the menus you submit to your food program correspond with your actual attendance. Some providers find that making a sign in–sign out log available to parents at drop-off and pickup times helps to maintain accurate attendance records.

Investing a little time each day can save you major headaches. You do not want to find yourself in a situation where you need to recreate required records from memory. If you must include documentation in children's files about unusual behaviors, accidents, or other relevant information, record your observations on the same day they occur.

Finally, do not procrastinate. If you find yourself overwhelmed or you have fallen behind in your record keeping, get help. Reach out to other providers or professionals who can give you suggestions on how to get started. Once your records are up to date and organized, you will feel a lot better about your program and much less apprehensive about potential visits.

CASE STUDY 2:
Maria Is Ready

It is Friday, and Maria is having a good day. She has operated her family child care program for approximately six months, and because of her good preparation, she feels confident and encouraged by how things have progressed so far.

Maria has a relatively small enrollment today because many of her children have had a bout of illness and are recuperating at home. Maria spoke with other providers before she developed her contract, and she wisely included a sick policy that appears to be working quite well. Maria accepts mildly ill children, but she will not accept a child who could infect other children in her program.

Maria has enrolled a new child, and because her contract requires that all paperwork be submitted before enrollment, the child's parents provided all the necessary paperwork in a timely fashion. Maria's own child, Angela, is home today because she is not feeling well. This doesn't affect Maria's family child care business because Maria understands the exception in her regulations that deals specifically with a provider's own child remaining at home, if necessary, without adversely affecting her quota.

When Maria happens to see her licensor walking up her driveway, she feels confident. She has anticipated this visit. Maria is well aware that her licensor must conduct an unannounced visit during the first six months of licensure, so Maria is prepared. Her required paperwork is organized and accessible. She is caring for an appropriate number of children and is not overenrolled. Maria is proud of her child care environment as well as her personal appearance. She can open her front door with a smile and confidence.

Checkpoints for Success

___ I have a good understanding of all the regulations, policies, contracts, and laws that pertain to the operation of my child care business.

___ I keep a copy of my child care regulations accessible during the hours I provide child care.

___ I am proactive and familiarize myself with the roles of the professionals who visit my home.

___ I have developed an effective provider-client contract that clearly communicates my expectations.

___ I stay current and upgrade my contract periodically.

___ I am organized, with ready access to all the required paperwork needed to operate my business.

COMMUNICATE EFFECTIVELY

As a provider, your ability to communicate directly reflects your confidence and ease in successfully getting your message across. The effective communication skills presented in this chapter will:

- increase the comfort level of those you are talking to
- go a long ways toward guaranteeing that your message is received
- assist you in accomplishing your goals and the goals of your business
- help to ensure retention of children

CASE STUDY 1:
Carmen's Inability to Speak Up

Carmen has only been a family child care provider for a little longer than a year. She currently cares for six children ages two to four. She is very enthusiastic about building her child care business. She puts a lot of thought into her curriculum and in planning each activity to make sure it is age appropriate for each child. The children are happy and engaged in Carmen's care, and she is proud of what she is doing.

Carmen has recently put together a winter curriculum. One of the objectives is to discuss hibernating animals. An activity for this objective is making caves for toy animals to sleep in using paper, glue, scissors, markers, and other art supplies.

Tanya has been a family child care monitor for fifteen years and each month visits the homes of providers who care for subsidized children— including Carmen's. Tanya has determined that the providers are not doing enough fine-motor skill activities with the children. She decided to distribute printed projects to the providers and require that they do the activities with the children. At Tanya's next monthly visit, she brought Carmen an activity sheet with directions for the children to make a planet mobile using paper, glue, scissors, markers, and so on. She told Carmen that she had to incorporate this activity into her schedule.

Upon receiving this news, Carmen could not think how a planet activity would fit into her curriculum. Carmen was so busy thinking of all the reasons that the activity would not work, she didn't even hear what Tanya was saying. Carmen knew that she had put a lot of thought into her activities and that they accomplished the same developmental goal as Tanya's activity. With her eyes lowered, Carmen softly started to tell Tanya that she was doing a similar activity.

Tanya looked at Carmen and thought, "She looks so uncertain. She really doesn't know what she is doing." Tanya concluded that Carmen was searching for an excuse for not doing her activity. She felt annoyed that Carmen, who had only been a provider for a short time, would question her ideas. With her arms crossed, Tanya bluntly told Carmen she did not want to hear excuses but wanted to see her do the activity as instructed.

Carmen felt frustrated that Tanya did not want to listen to her. She felt that Tanya was pushing her to do things Tanya's way. Because Carmen thought that Tanya looked angry, she did not confront Tanya with the way she was feeling. She agreed to do the activity that Tanya presented.

Carmen knew that her activities were fulfilling the children's developmental goals in all the learning domains. She wanted to speak up for herself, but she didn't know how to handle Tanya's strong personality.

When Tanya left, Carmen felt very frustrated and unsatisfied with the way the visit went.

CHALLENGE: Presenting Ideas Clearly

Every time you communicate with another person, you encounter that person's nonverbal communication in the form of body language—and your own body language adds to the communication. What we feel inside is often reflected in how we move, our facial expressions, how we stand, even our subtle gestures. Sometimes the words and the body language match, but other times they do not. And there are times when our body language may hinder our ability to get our ideas across to the other person clearly.

One of the ways that Carmen failed to present her curriculum idea clearly was by not looking in Tanya's eyes. Carmen's body language conveyed to Tanya that she was uncertain about what she was saying. Yet Carmen was not aware of how her body language was being interpreted by Tanya.

SOLUTION: Match Body Language to Message

As a business owner, there are many times when you need to get your message across to clients or other visitors. Learning to pay attention to body language will help you become more aware of how you communicate. And it will help you change your body language so you communicate in a clear and effective manner. The study of body language is very complex. Many researchers have studied for years the subtle signs people display and how that impacts communication. Researcher Albert Mehrabian found that when communicating our emotions or attitudes, words account for only 7 percent of our communication, whereas tone of voice and inflection (38 percent) and body language (55 percent) account for the majority of our communication (*Silent Messages*, 1981, Wadsworth). Another researcher, anthropologist Ray Birdwhistell, estimated that humans can produce up to 250,000 facial expressions (Pease and Pease, *The Definitive Book of Body Language*, 2004, Bantam)—and each of those can have a variety of interpretations and misinterpretations!

You have a diverse population of visitors who range from parents with different backgrounds and cultures to professionals who come into your home for safety, regulatory, mentoring, observational, and contractual reasons. Each has a unique agenda and feelings of authority. When you need to communicate a message that is important to you but may require the other person to change his thinking, the interaction can be difficult.

DEFENSIVENESS

Often a request can cause the recipient to become defensive. In the case study, Tanya became defensive because she thought Carmen was trying to make excuses for not using her activity. Once a person becomes defensive, she will not listen to the message. Instead, she will be concentrating on formulating her defense. Knowing the signs that a person is becoming defensive would have helped Carmen. She could have looked for clues like these:

- turning her body away from you
- looking down
- crossing her arms
- showing little facial expression
- clenching her hands

Carmen needed to pay attention to her own body language as well. She needed to make sure that she was not exhibiting signs of defensiveness. (Go back to the case study and look for clues that she was, in fact, defensive.) Carmen would have communicated better if she had displayed receptive, open, and comfortable body language. If Carmen had been more confident and comfortable with her message, Tanya would have been more receptive.

RECEPTIVENESS

When you need to get your message across, carefully watch the other person's reaction to what you are saying. If the conversation seems to be turning negative, check your own body language, tone of voice, facial expression, and eye contact. Try to show that you are open to continuing a true dialogue with the person. Receptive body language includes the following:

- eye contact
- hands relaxed in your lap or open on the table
- body facing the other person and/or tilting slightly toward him
- relaxed facial expression, smile

SOLUTION: Interpret Others' Body Language Carefully

Body language can mean different things in various cultures and ethnic groups, and from person to person. Before you label a person aggressive or defensive, watch her natural habits and mannerisms while you are talking to her about a nonconfrontational issue, because doing so helps establish a baseline. You should never jump to conclusions when interpreting body language, especially when you are just beginning to learn to recognize non-verbal cues. Asking more questions and probing more deeply may validate—or overturn—your interpretations. Also consider what you know about the person's personality. For example, a visitor might feel more comfortable when she crosses her arms. Another might touch her ears and chin or play with her hair, even when she is comfortable. Learning these natural mannerisms helps you interpret body language more accurately.

Understanding body language takes a lot of practice. Take advantage of occasions when you can sit back and watch people. Try to identify some subtle and nonsubtle actions and reactions. Look for the way a person positions her head. Watch the movement of her eyes, hands, feet, and legs, and how she places her body. Do not accuse a person of the behavior simply because you observe some of these gestures. Be quick to observe and slow to interpret, since assumptions can often cause more miscommunication than they solve. Nevertheless, body language can offer some clues to prompt more questions and to probe more deeply to avoid miscommunication.

CHALLENGE: Dealing with Different Communication Styles

As a family child care provider, you are an independent business owner and must communicate with many different personalities. Therefore, understanding the communication process and the different ways people communicate is very important to the success of your business. Many problems that occur are the result of a failure of communication between you and clients or other individuals who visit your home for business, inspection, regulatory, or observational purposes.

In the case study, Carmen was confronted with a very strong communication style. She did not know how to communicate with Tanya, so she agreed to fit Tanya's activity into her curriculum. This left her frustrated.

SOLUTION: Learn to Recognize and Communicate with Different Styles

When a sender transmits an idea to a receiver, that is communication. Effective communication occurs only if the receiver understands what the sender intended to transmit. When you speak to parents and other visitors, they receive two types of information: content and context.

> **Content** is the actual words or symbols of the message, whether you give the information orally or in written form. Some words are used and interpreted differently. In addition, some words have multiple meanings, which can further confuse the message. Therefore, even though you know what you are saying, various people will understand your message differently. Even the simplest message can be misunderstood. In the case study, Tanya interpreted Carmen's message as an excuse rather than a statement of fact.

> **Context** is the way the message is delivered. It includes the tone of voice, the look in the sender's eyes, body language, hand gestures, and emotions (anger, fear, uncertainty, confidence, etc.). Context often causes messages to be misunderstood, because people commonly believe what they see rather than what they hear. Recipients are more likely to trust the accuracy of nonverbal than verbal behaviors. Even though Carmen was confident about her curriculum, her body language and tone of voice did not convey that confidence.

Have you ever wondered why you seem to "click" with some people while others frustrate you? Have you found that what works with one person does not necessarily work with another? The reason is simple. Everyone is unique. Everyone has a particular personality and way of interacting with people.

Occasionally, your style of communication may directly conflict with some-one else's, making your message difficult to get across. Learning to see how your style of communication interacts with the styles of others can give you a greater understanding of clients' and visitors' negative or positive responses. You need people to know that you understand them. Whether you agree with their points of view or not, you open the door to communication by validating their feelings.

As you read about the following communication styles, try to identify your own style, and think about Carmen and Tanya and how their styles clashed. Notice that certain combinations of styles do tend to conflict with each other.

INDEPENDENT IRMA

Independent Irma often makes quick decisions, and she tends to talk fast. Irma may be a poor listener. She can easily see the big picture and becomes impatient with those who do not. In the case study, Tanya was like Irma. She decided to implement curriculum activities without even acknowledging what her providers were doing. Irma might have provided services for many years; she might believe that she already knows everything you have to tell her. She can be tactless and willingly state that she does not need you to tell her anything, because she is capable of doing things by herself.

So, how can you accommodate Irma's communication style? When talk-ing to Irma, stick to the subject. Do not add a lot of unnecessary informa-tion. Remember that a person like Irma believes she can do a better job than others, so she will not welcome your opinion on how something should be done. You need to acknowledge Irma's years of experience and ask for her input to achieve any goal you are trying to reach. By discussing options with her and deciding collaboratively on a course of action, you validate Irma's abilities and years of experience.

In the case study, Carmen could have said, "I can see your activity is designed to encourage the development of fine-motor skills. I had planned to do a different activity that uses the same skills. Could you look at it and give me your opinion?" Reviewing the activity together, with Carmen acknowledging Tanya's years of experience, would have opened the lines of communication to a discussion of the goals of each activity—and a resolution that was comfortable to both Carmen and Tanya.

CHATTY CATHY

This type of person loves people and loves to talk. Cathy is the person who will tell you her life history and the history of everyone else in her family. Cathy likes to make jokes, and it is hard to get her to take your conversation seriously. She is expressive and fun, and she loves to be the center of attention.

How do you accommodate Cathy's communication style? When you have something important to discuss with Cathy, you might be tempted to get right to the point. However, you should spend a few minutes socializing; this is important to Cathy. But you must limit socializing and take control of the conversation. Cathy likes a lot of praise and acknowledgment. If the conversation is off track, you might be able to turn it around to your purpose by commenting positively about the way she hugs her child good-bye everyday, or if she's a coach, on how helpful her suggestion was last month.

Many times a parent with Cathy's style feels overwhelmed with work and parenting. Cathy does not like to feel as though she is working alone. When proposing new ideas or changes to her, use plural pronouns—"Let us" or "we"—instead of "you."

For example, suppose that you have been working with Cathy's child to be toilet trained. The child lets you know when he needs the bathroom and stays dry all day. Yet each morning he comes in a diaper, and Cathy has expressed to you that it is easier for her to put a diaper on the child. Then she does not have to worry about accidents or taking the child to the bathroom if she is out. You tell Cathy that you appreciate how clean she always brings her son, and then you suggest working together to help her son appreciate being clean by going to the toilet instead of in his diaper. Together you discuss ways to encourage the child when he is at home. Each day when Cathy brings her son, you discuss the progress. And you follow up with a phone call during the weekend to see how Cathy is handling the training of her son. When they arrive on Monday and he's wearing underwear, you are excited and offer lots of praise to both Cathy and her son.

AGREEABLE ANNIE

Annie is laid back. She does not like confrontation and often agrees with you just to avoid an argument. Annie is a good listener and is sensitive to others. As a child care provider, her sensitivity can cause problems because she tries to balance pleasing every parent with complying with every regulation. Annie generally will not tell you how she really feels. Nor will she ask for help. She does not make decisions quickly; she needs time to think things over. Annie has a hard time saying no and may agree to a task or change she does not fully understand or finds difficult to accomplish.

Do you recognize Annie? In the case study, Carmen communicates in this style. Occasionally you will encounter parents that communicate in this style. When talking with Annie, you need to be especially careful not to ask yes/no questions. Instead, ask questions that will elicit a detailed response. When instituting a policy or procedure, go over each part of the instructions and make sure Annie fully understands it. If paperwork is needed, give Annie a plan to get the paperwork completed within a certain time frame. Remember that when Annie needs help, she probably will not ask for it.

For example, imagine that the weather is getting cold but you still like to take the children out for a short time each day for fresh air. You ask families to remember to bring hats and mittens for each child. Annie repeatedly brings her child without the proper clothing for outdoor play, so you cannot take any of the children out. In trying to rectify this situation, you should first give Annie the reasons why it is important for her to bring outdoor clothing.

Make sure she understands that all the children have to stay in when she fails to bring outdoor clothes. After giving Annie the reason, do not ask, "Do you understand?" If you ask the question that way, Annie will most likely respond, "Yes." Instead, ask her for specifics, "How can I help you plan to make sure you bring the winter clothing?" You might have to keep asking questions until you know she has a plan in place to meet your request. If there is any part that is not clear, offer suggestions, such as putting the clothes in the child's bag the night before or buying an extra hat and mittens to leave at child care. When you are convinced that Annie understands, confirm the plan for action: "So you can start tomorrow. That's great!"

FACTUAL FRED

People like Fred are very cautious. Fred likes to get all the facts and details before he acts or speaks. Often Fred can be a perfectionist. He does not show emotion, so you may find it difficult to know what he is thinking. How can you accommodate Fred's communication style? Fred needs to know the facts and reasons behind any comments or decisions you make. Conduct your research before you discuss any issues with Fred. Have copies of information such as documents or policies that substantiate your point of view. Doing this will ensure that Fred will be more receptive. Remember, he does not necessarily want your opinion on how something should be done, but he will respect facts that back up your request.

For example, you might have Fred as your licensor. He has told you that he does not like to see the TV on at all during child care hours. He has instituted a policy among the providers he visits that does not allow any TV watching. However, you have found an educational program that encourages social development. This month, each thirty-minute program is about sharing. You sit with the children to watch the program and then discuss what they saw and conduct activities that encourage sharing. When discussing with Fred your inclusion of this TV watching, do not say, "I *think* the children can benefit from watching this program." Fred is not interested in your opinion. He might not *think* the children are benefiting from this program. Instead, refer to your prepared facts and any information you have copied for him. Say, "Look at these facts about the quality and benefits of this program. You can see why I am putting it into my curriculum."

SOLUTION: Know Your Own Communication Style

Just as important as recognizing how Independent Irma, Chatty Cathy, Agreeable Annie, and Factual Fred communicate is knowing your own style. Answer the following questions.

How quickly do you grasp information? Think about how you learn, because how you learn is most likely how you communicate ideas. If it takes you awhile to understand directions or new procedures, you most likely empathize with others who need a little extra time from you to explain what you want them to do. However, this approach can annoy a person who easily grasps the picture and resents your explaining it over and over again.

How talkative are you? Do you talk to people everywhere you go? If you are very talkative, you might frustrate the person who wants you to get to the point. The reverse can also be true. The person who wants to talk about everything and does not concentrate on your message might frustrate you.

Are you a morning person? If you think best in the morning and want to have a deep conversation with a client who is a night person, both of you can become frustrated because you are not giving the conversation the same level of attention.

Do you avoid unpleasant situations and conflicts? The fact is that you will find yourself in situations that are unpleasant. You might even have to face an aggressive visitor or client. You need to practice how to use your skills to handle uncomfortable situations. If the other person can sense your uncertainty, that person will try to gain control of the situation.

Do you believe people want to hear what you have to say? Your confidence is reflected in your communication with others. Believing in your message and in your ability to get the message across to someone else is one key to effective communication.

Do you voice your opinion, or do you keep your thoughts to yourself? Your job is to assure the health and safety of children in your care. If you do not normally speak up, you might find it difficult to speak up when it is necessary. Practice voicing your opinion to people with whom you feel comfortable.

Do you share all of your thoughts, or do you keep them to yourself? People who keep their thoughts to themselves might not be effective communicators. On the other hand, people who talk before thinking might not communicate productively either. Both of these styles can cause the recipients to become frustrated. Learn to strike a balance between voicing your thoughts when it is important and keeping your thoughts to yourself to avoid confrontation. This is a skill that must be practiced.

Do you become overwhelmed when people talk at a rapid pace? If you do, you need to ask the person you are speaking with to slow down. Repeat what you are hearing to make sure you understand what is being said. If you tend to talk fast, make an effort to slow down, especially when you are explaining new information.

When answering questions, do you give detailed answers or short, pointed answers? Find out how your answers are perceived by others. Know which people need more information and which ones are only looking for short answers. Then, adjust your communication style as needed.

These questions require thoughtful self-reflection to answer. If you take the time to answer them truthfully, your reflections will give you a better idea of how you communicate. Once you identify the style that best describes how you communicate, match it to the style of the people you deal with on a regular basis.

SOLUTION: Manage Conflicts Between Styles

Conflicts are most likely to occur when you and a recipient have different communication styles. The following chart presents potential conflicts between several communication styles. When examining these conflicts, think about the strategy you would use for better interactions with the people who communicate differently. Determine why a conflict exists and what you need to change to communicate more effectively.

PROVIDER'S STYLE	VISITOR'S STYLE	CONFLICT
Impatient Irma: talks fast, makes quick decisions, is blunt and impatient	**Chatty Cathy:** talkative and social, loves to joke, is very expressive	**Provider:** Feels impatient and may be too blunt with client. **Visitor:** Feels uncomfortable, tries to make a joke, makes provider more impatient.
Chatty Cathy: sociable, likes to joke, talks a lot about personal business	**Impatient Irma:** makes quick decisions	**Provider:** May take up too much time being social. **Visitor:** Feels impatient because she has a lot of things to do when she leaves. May respond bluntly or tactlessly, causing provider to become more social or make more jokes to win over client.
Impatient Irma: talks fast, is blunt and impatient, sees whole picture	**Factual Fred:** needs to hear facts before making decisions	**Provider:** May feel impatient with client's questions and lack of support for his ideas. May not understand that client does not see whole picture. **Visitor:** Feels provider is trying to push him into doing something he does not fully understand. May resent provider for not giving sufficient reasons or information. Differences may lead to frustration for provider and client.

Conflicts Between Styles chart, continued

PROVIDER'S STYLE	VISITOR'S STYLE	CONFLICT
Factual Fred: looks at all facts, is detail oriented	**Impatient Irma:** sees big picture, makes quick decisions, is poor listener	**Provider:** Tries to present all facts and details about topic or goal. **Visitor:** May become impatient because she quickly grasps the big picture and understands what provider is trying to communicate. Direct conflict between these two communication styles leads to frustration and breakdown in communication on both sides.
Agreeable Annie: avoids conflict, wants people to like her, has difficulty saying no	**Impatient Irma:** tactless, demanding, impatient	**Provider:** Has difficulty discussing corrections or problems with client, particularly if corrections involve difficult measures (like termination for nonpayment); may feel overwhelmed and unable to handle issues needing discussion, creating an argument. **Visitor:** May respond bluntly and tactlessly, steering conversations away from the point of the message.
Factual Fred: detail oriented, well prepared before speaking, may be perfectionist	**Agreeable Annie:** introverted, avoids confrontation, does not voice her feelings	**Provider:** Well prepared with details. May not recognize how client feels. **Visitor:** May not agree with provider yet nods her head in agreement to avoid confrontation. Provider's perfectionism can make client feel inadequate. Provider and client miss opportunities to identify problems and reach resolutions.

CHALLENGE: Listening Effectively

Listening and hearing are different actions. You might hear people talking in the next booth at a restaurant. Although you can physically hear the sounds, unless your brain is registering the words and the meaning of the words, you are not really listening. Effective listening requires more than simply hearing. Good listening takes preparation and practice. And it is worth it! Listening involves connecting with a person and making him feel comfortable.

In the case study, Carmen was not listening to Tanya's suggestion because she was absorbed in thinking about her own curriculum. Carmen needed to listen to what Tanya was saying in order to turn this confrontation into a collaboration that used the best of both ideas for curriculum.

SOLUTION: Listen Actively

Often when a client or other visitor comes to your child care, the children sense you are distracted and can become excited and lively. During this hectic time you may hear what is being said, but you might not register what is being said. If important information is being communicated, you need to be concerned with whether both you and the visitor can hear *and* listen.

Drop-off and pickup times can be especially hectic. Yet you might need to tell a parent some important information about his child or discuss a problem with your licensor. Be careful that you do not become so focused on your message and making sure that you say everything you need to say. You do not want to miss the important cues telling you whether your message has been received correctly. You need to make sure that your message does not become more important than what the other person has to say. Make sure you do not do all the talking. Give the other person a chance to speak. Your goal is to make sure the person understands your instructions or information. Listening skills are important to your achieving this goal.

Avoid giving the impression that you do not value what the other person has to say. Evaluate yourself and keep the following suggestions in mind:

- Do not look at your watch or the door when the other person is speaking.
- Do not continually interrupt the other person with your opinion.
- Do not avoid eye contact.
- Do not fidget or play with paperwork while the other person is speaking.

- Do not make inappropriate facial expressions.

- Do not pay more attention to what you are going to say next than to listening to what the other person is saying.

Listening to others and giving them a chance to speak does not mean that you agree with them. Acknowledging their point of view shows them respect and support and helps build a relationship in which differences can be openly discussed.

Listening can be especially difficult when a client disagrees with or complains about your child care services, or when a regulator complains about your paperwork. You might have heard this same complaint or excuse many times, which can make it difficult to listen again. But you must. Listening carefully to what the other person says can help you determine what she wants. She might be venting and complaining, while at the bottom, she wants something to change. Try to discern what the other person is really asking for. To do so, you must ask questions that draw out the person's feelings. For example, do not ask, "Why do you feel that way?" A "why" question can put the person on the defensive. Instead, ask, "When did you start to feel this way?" or "What bothers you the most about this situation?" Acknowledge her answers with good eye contact. Lean forward, do not interrupt, and occasionally nod your head to show you are listening.

Do not always give your opinion. A visitor might be upset about something that in your opinion is trivial, but recognize that the problem is not trivial to her. Resist saying, "I don't think you should let that bother you." Instead, ask, "How do you feel about . . . ?"

Taking time to identify and validate the other's feelings is called active listening. Use this skill to make sure you fully and clearly understand what the other person is saying. The key to successful active listening is sincere interest in understanding what the other person is feeling. If your goal is to understand her feelings, you must concentrate on what she is saying and make sure you understand it before you speak.

You might believe that the person is saying one thing to you, and yet the next minute she is saying something else. To alleviate any misunderstanding or confusion, restate what you have heard: "To make sure I understand you correctly, I hear you saying . . ." Rephrase and paraphrase. Do not add your own opinions or concerns. Listen and verify your perception of what the person is telling you.

Once you have defined and clarified the problem, try to identify the feeling she is expressing. This can be done by saying, "You feel *[identify the feeling]* because *[state the action]*." For example, "You feel angry because I am not welcoming your curriculum activities." If you are unsure of the person's underlying issue, ask more probing questions to understand what she is really saying. For example, "I would like to understand more about why you feel the way you do. Are the activities necessary to complete or are the developmental outcomes for the children more important to you?"

Before the two of you can come to an agreeable solution, the other person must understand your perspective. Using "I messages" is a good way to help her understand your perspective without becoming confrontational. You can let her know you have listened to what she has said and that the situation affects you differently. "I messages" do not place blame. They create an atmosphere for problem solving and positive communication. "I messages" have three parts:

1. **Your feelings.** State feeling: "I feel discouraged. . . ."
2. **The situation causing the feeling.** State the other person's behavior: "when you don't look at my curriculum."
3. **Your request.** State what you want to happen: "I want to show you my curriculum so you can see we have similar outcomes and goals."

Examine the difference between using the above "I message" and saying this: "You make me discouraged because you never validate what I am doing with the children or even look at my activities." Notice how using "I messages" takes the confrontation out of the communication.

This is not always easy, but once you let the person know that you understand her problem, and she understands yours, you can work together toward a solution. Understanding each other's position and respecting each side of the issue often lead to finding a middle ground that is agreeable and workable for both of you.

CASE STUDY 2:
Carmen Respectfully Explains Her Ideas

Last week when Tanya visited Carmen for their monthly coaching session, she insisted that Carmen use her curriculum activity to support children's fine-motor skills. Carmen felt very strongly that her curriculum was meeting the developmental goals for each child and she did not need Tanya's activity. Carmen was very frustrated that she had not been able to effectively communicate with Tanya how proud and confident she felt that her curriculum was meeting the same goals as the activity Tanya presented.

Carmen knew that Tanya had a very strong personality and that she often talked fast and made quick decisions. She knew that Tanya did not always take the time to listen to others. Carmen also acknowledged that she often found it hard to confront others and would rather agree than cause any problems. Furthermore, Carmen knew she hadn't really listened to Tanya's reasons for requiring that the activities be conducted. She was disappointed and frustrated, so she decided to make a plan for the next visit.

Carmen carefully thought about how she would present her curriculum to Tanya. She also thought about the possible ways Tanya could respond. She then thought about how she would handle each response.

A few weeks later, Tanya came to conduct her monthly visit. Expecting to hear excuses, Tanya narrowed her eyes as she handed Carmen a new activity. She asked Carmen whether she had conducted the activity from last month with the children. Carmen took the papers and, with a relaxed posture, met Tanya's eyes as she said, "Yes, I did. I understand how concerned you are that the children are missing some of the important learning domains. I want to make sure that I am meeting all the developmental goals for the children. You have so much experience. Would you please look at my curriculum and let me know what you think?"

Tanya immediately looked at Carmen and relaxed her facial expression. She was pleased that Carmen acknowledged her years of experience, and she agreed to examine the curriculum. She was very impressed to see that Carmen had identified developmental goals for each child and scheduled activities that addressed each child's goals.

Carmen then asked Tanya if she would show her how to fit Tanya's activities into her curriculum for the month. Tanya pointed out specific skills that her activity addressed and recognized that Carmen's curriculum activities addressed the same skills. Tanya made some suggestions and encouraged Carmen to use her own activities instead of those that Tanya brought.

When Tanya left, Carmen felt validated. She also felt excited to implement some of the suggestions Tanya had made. Tanya felt encouraged to see that one of her providers was working so hard at providing quality child care. Both women look forward to the next visit.

Checkpoints for Success

Learning effective communication skills takes practice and self-examination. If communication with a visitor goes wrong, do not automatically blame the other person. You own your child care business; the success or failure of the business is your responsibility. Therefore, it is your responsibility to accommodate your style of communication to the client or other person visiting your home. You should not expect the others to accommodate your style. Each time someone comes to your home or you need to convey a message to a parent, think about whether it was a negative or positive communication. Use the following checklist to help you identify your strengths and weaknesses. Doing so gives you an opportunity to think about what you could have done differently.

___ I used communication skills well on this visit.

___ I facilitated the communication positively.

___ I listened carefully and was able to discern the other person's feelings.

___ I was aware of my body language.

___ I felt that my goals for the interaction were achieved.

MAINTAIN A POSITIVE ATTITUDE

Your attitude is driven by how you feel about something. We have the choice of whether we will face each day with a negative or a positive attitude. Our choice is reflected in negative or positive outcomes to our interactions with others.

CASE STUDY 1:
Simone's Confrontational Disaster

Simone has been a family child care provider for ten years. She has put a lot of thought and work into her child care environment, which is in a large family room at the back of the house. With sliding glass doors and big windows, the room shines with natural light. The child care room is right next to the kitchen and bathroom for meals and toileting. Next to the kitchen, at the front of her house, is her living room. She can see through the kitchen to the front door, which opens directly into the living room. In the past, families and visitors to her business have used the front door rather than walked around to the back door, which leads into the family room.

A few months ago, Simone installed new carpeting in her living room and asked all families and visitors to use the "child care door" in the back. Most have complied. However, one visitor, Kara, who comes monthly to monitor the children who receive state subsidies, continues to use the front door. On Kara's last visit, Simone tried to talk to her about using the child care door, and Kara just brushed her off, saying, "Oh, yeah, if I remember." Simone was very frustrated and found it hard to conceal her feelings.

Today the children are seated around the kitchen table, busily engaged in a craft project. It is raining. Simone looks up to see Kara sloshing through the puddles on her way up the front walk. Soon, even though Simone has posted a small sign beside the bell saying to please use the child care door in the back, Kara is ringing the doorbell. Simone believes that Kara is deliberately going to the front door, ignoring her wishes, and she becomes very aggravated. Simone knows that because she accepts children with state subsidies, she is required to submit to these monthly visits. But she also feels that she has the right to designate what door the visitor should use.

As Simone walks to the door, her frustration grows. When she opens the door, she stands with her arms crossed and, glaring at Kara, says, "Didn't you see the sign? Don't you remember that I've asked you to use the back door?" Kara says simply, "I forgot."

Simone doesn't like Kara's attitude and feels that Kara is taking the situation too lightly. She says tersely, "Well, you need to go around to the back."

Kara says, "Look, I'm not going around back. It's raining out. You need to let me in, or I will cite you for refusing a visit."

By now, Simone is becoming very angry at Kara's attitude. She feels that Kara doesn't care about her request and has no intention of ever using the back door. Simone stands her ground and says, "Well, cite me, because you are not coming in this door."

Kara immediately reacts to what she feels was Simone's unreasonable attitude. "That's exactly what I will do," she says, and angrily strides back to her car.

Simone shuts the door and stands against it, feeling she has won but resentful that she has been put into a position that may result in negative consequences. For the rest of the day, she dwells on the confrontation. Her mood matches the rainy, miserable day; she shows little patience for the children. At the end of the day, she is left exhausted, stressed, and dreading the next confrontation. She grumbles, "Why do these things always happen to me?"

CHALLENGE: Handling Confrontations

As a provider, you interact with children and their families, monitors, inspectors, and representatives from regulatory agencies. Each adult holds a measure of authority over you and your child care business. Occasionally you will encounter a regulatory individual or parent who does not listen to you, is very demanding, and/or displays a negative attitude toward you. It is difficult to remain positive when you are interacting with someone who seems to be looking for things to criticize.

SOLUTION: Control Your Responses

Knowing your own attitude—how you feel about something—is key. Your attitude greatly affects how you interact with others. If you have a negative attitude, the outcome of your interactions is likely to be negative. In contrast, a positive attitude usually results in positive outcomes. Does having a positive attitude mean that you only think happy thoughts? No! The reality is that not every day of caring for children is filled with wonder, delight, and laughter. It's difficult to think happy thoughts when you don't feel well, when the children don't feel well, when the children cannot seem to hold on to a glass of milk without spilling, when a parent forgot to bring diapers, and when your food program monitor is at the door.

After her confrontation with Kara, Simone has two choices. She can react pessimistically, with a negative attitude, or she can choose a positive attitude and a proactive approach. Because Simone thinks that bad things always happen *to* her, Simone is obviously moving in the negative direction.

When you have a negative confrontation, do you dwell on what went wrong? A pessimistic person dwells on the negative, turning every situation into a poor-me story. Admittedly, you do not always have control over what happens to you during the day. You do, however, have control over how you deal with it. Choose a positive approach.

At the end of each day, find something that is positive instead of dwelling on what went wrong. For example: *I saw Brian share his blocks with Megan; he's finally learning!* Or *My reminders are starting to work.* Or *Sara wanted me to have the picture she drew. She was really proud of it.* Working with children, you accumulate many positive events each day that bring you joy. Never let one person or situation take that joy away by dwelling on negative events. If Simone had maintained a positive attitude toward Kara during the visit and for the rest of her day, she might have been able to enjoy the positive learning the children displayed on that rainy day.

SOLUTION: Respond Effectively to Passive-Aggressive Behavior

Some people behave passive-aggressively. Passive-aggressive behavior includes seeming agreement with your requests followed by indirect resistance, contradictory actions, and avoidance of confrontation about the behavior. Passive-aggressive behavior might include procrastination or failure to carry out your request effectively. Such actions can produce the opposite of what you requested.

You see this behavior when a parent agrees to what you ask her to do, but then she actually doesn't do it. A passive-aggressive person has plenty of excuses:

- "I tried, but I don't know how to do it."
- "I meant to do it, but I forgot."
- "It's not my fault because *[someone or some situation kept me from carrying out the request]*."
- "I was going to do it next week."
- "It's not fair! I don't know why they *[authority]* want me to do this."

Passive-aggressive behavior comes swathed in excuses that may trigger your own guilt for having made the request. In the case study, Kara exhibited passive-aggressive behavior when she claimed to have forgotten Simone's requests. Then she tried to make Simone feel guilty for expecting her to go the extra distance in the rain.

Consider this example: a parent says, "I know I told you I would pick up my child's medical report from the doctor's office for you, but I just ran out of time. My mother is sick, and I had to bring her supper. By the time I did that, the office had closed. I know you would not have wanted me to make my mother wait." The parent's answer not only excuses her own responsibility, but it also assigns responsibility to you for ensuring that the mom got her meal on time.

When you identify a person who behaves passive-aggressively, you have some positive choices. Ask a question after making your request so the person must give you feedback on how she is really feeling. Here are three questions you might ask the parent who didn't bring in the paperwork:

- "What are your options for getting the necessary paperwork?" (fax, pick up, mail)
- "Do you fully understand why this paperwork is necessary?"
- "Do you understand the consequences of not submitting the paperwork?"

When you ask a question, give the person time to answer. Even if she is behaving negatively and complaining, you need to listen respectfully. After you have heard her comments, excuses, or complaints, do not respond in a demeaning or sarcastic manner. Remember to control your body language. If you roll your eyes or cross your arms, you send negative and disapproving signals. Instead, acknowledge what you have heard. You might say, "I understand how you are feeling." Or you might ask more questions.

Once you have listened and understood her, restate what you need and why it is necessary for her to take responsibility. In the case of the mother who did not bring in the needed paperwork, do not allow her to manipulate you into taking responsibility for getting the paperwork. Do not do the work for her. Clearly define your and her responsibilities. Here's how you might deal effectively with her passive-aggressive behavior.

When the mother arrives the next day without the paperwork, listen to her feedback. Remain neutral while she makes her excuses. Then say, "I would love to keep your child in my child care. You understand the regulatory requirements about the paperwork that needs to be submitted when your child enters care. Let's see if we can come up with a workable solution so that I can get the paperwork today."

By responding in a direct, nonaccusatory way, you get your point across without humiliating her. Chances are, you will see the results that you need. And how did it all begin? With a positive attitude!

Practice maintaining a positive attitude, and you will reap the rewards. Positive attitudes have been linked with many benefits, physical and mental.

When you have a positive attitude, you are

- generally more motivated to solve a problem, change a situation, or just get through a bad day
- relieving stress
- able to look at accomplishing a task as a challenge instead of a chore
- instilling confidence in others
- helping your overall physical and mental health
- happier

In contrast, negativity drains your energy and can lead to more negativity.

CHALLENGE: Remaining Assertive

Family child care providers are by nature very nurturing people. In order to operate your business effectively, you also need to be assertive. Nurturing and being assertive are not mutually exclusive. You are operating your own business. All business owners, whether running a restaurant, retail store, or service company, must assertively meet contractual and regulatory standards.

So what does it mean to be assertive? It's often confused with being aggressive, but they are not the same. Assertive people use bold or confident statements and behavior. In contrast, people who behave aggressively tend to be forceful or hostile, especially when intended to dominate or master. Assertive individuals try to understand others and acknowledge the value that others bring to a situation. In a conflict, they listen actively, explain themselves clearly, and invite others to work with them toward a solution. People who behave aggressively are defensive and oppositional. Assertive people recognize that to work successfully with others, they must not anger or humiliate them. Examine some more specific differences here:

ASSERTIVE BEHAVIOR

promotes negotiation	is a win-win approach
promotes problem solving	is goal oriented
promotes good relationships	promotes trust
is direct and respectful	

AGGRESSIVE BEHAVIOR

promotes anger	is a win-lose approach
promotes negative consequences	is controlling
makes demands	promotes resentment
is direct and tactless	

Assertive behavior promotes positive relationships by taking the feelings of others into account. Aggressive behavior might appear to solve problems, but it actually promotes feelings of humiliation and resentment. It should never be viewed as successful.

SOLUTION: Turn Confrontations into Collaborations

Confrontations can be hard, but there are times when they are necessary. The key is to turn them into opportunities for collaboration. This requires a measure of assertiveness on your part. Your attitude plays a major role in being successfully assertive.

If you anticipate a negative reaction when you enter a tough situation, you might come across negatively from the beginning. In the case study, Simone's attitude set the tone for the entire visit. You can help set a cooperative and positive tone by examining your own comfort with assertiveness. Know your personality. Which description below best fits you?

- **Passive:** You don't feel you have the right to be heard. You often feel uncomfortable expressing yourself, fearful that you will not like the response you receive. You are usually willing to back down to avoid conflict.
- **Assertive:** You are comfortable expressing what you think. You can express your views without stepping on others, without anger or attack. Your goal is to find a resolution that works for everyone.
- **Aggressive:** You stand up for yourself, even at the expense of others. You use tactics like a loud voice, sarcasm, and forcefulness to get your way.

In order to understand your attitude, you need to step back and think about your personality. When you use aggression, you might feel satisfied because you've achieved your goal. However, you need to think about the other person's feelings; using aggressive tactics makes the other person feel uncomfortable, angry, even intimidated. In the case of Simone and Kara, both became angry. Instead of focusing on the message, each focused on her own feelings.

SOLUTION: Be Aware of How You Are Coming Across

If you want to be assertive, you have to *feel* assertive. The other person must see and feel your assertiveness too. Remember to present yourself as assertive in all of the following ways.

EYE CONTACT

To maintain a positive attitude and master assertive skills, use direct eye contact that tells others you need to be listened to. Avoid staring and glaring, which are aggressive behaviors. Achieving the appropriate amount of eye contact takes practice. When you engage in direct eye contact, occasionally look away so that you don't make the other person uncomfortable. Looking away periodically does not mean you avoid her eyes altogether. If you avoid her eyes and look down, your behavior implies that you are uncomfortable with your message. Similarly, looking past the person to the door or to the side conveys the message that you really do not want to be there. One solution is to glance at the children or paperwork.

FACIAL EXPRESSIONS AND BODY LANGUAGE

Make sure your facial expressions and body language fit the message you are attempting to convey. Try to keep your expression relaxed. Do not lean toward the other person; this is an aggressive stance. There is a difference between leaning toward a person in interest and leaning toward a person with an aggressive stance. When a person is interested in what you say, their body is more relaxed and their chin is tucked in. When displaying an aggressive stance, the chin is generally lifted and protruding. The body is tense, the arms may be crossed, or fists may be clenched. Try to sit or stand at her same level. For example, if she is sitting down and you are standing, she might feel you are looking down on her. Try to remain at eye level and be respectful of her personal space. Always be mindful of keeping a comfortable distance and not crowding the other person. Do not fidget. Relax your body as much as you can. In the case study, Simone stood with her arms crossed and blocked the door. This is a clear example of aggressive body language. (See chapter 4 for more information about body language.)

TONE OF VOICE

Pay attention to the tone and volume of your voice. Make sure you don't sound angry, overly loud, patronizing, or too soft. Often when people are nervous, they speak too fast. Practice what you want to say so you can control your speech. Be careful not to raise the tone of your voice at the end of a statement; this makes you sound as if you are uncertain and asking a question instead of making a statement.

CLEAR LANGUAGE

Know in advance what your objectives are. State them in clear, understandable language. Do not use words, acronyms, or jargon that could be unfamiliar. Organize your presentation. Concentrate on making your objective rather than the person the target of your conversation.

LISTEN

Allow the other person to state her opinion. This shows respect. While acknowledging her right to feel the way she does, you should remain firm—especially when your objective concerns regulatory or contractual issues.

SOLUTION: Use Assertive Language

When you want to be assertive, what you say and how you say it determine how well your message is conveyed. You need to make sure that your message concentrates on goals and not on the other person's faults. Don't think of assertiveness as winning or losing. Instead, look at it as a way to negotiate a solution to a problem. Remember: even though you might be in the position to enforce regulations, such as requiring paperwork from parents, or to establish rules for your business, such as which door to use to enter your home, you and the parent or regulator must be a team working together toward a common goal.

Do not start a discussion with "You," "You never," or "You always." These words are likely to put the other person on the defensive immediately. Words like *never* and *always* set you up for debate and argument. When you use such generalizations, you shift the focus away from your objective. The other person will try to defend herself by coming up with counterexamples, and the focus shifts to accusations and defenses. When a person can refute your generalizations, she weakens your position and strengthens her own. Keep statements fact-based. For example, if you say to a visitor, "You are never on time," she will likely respond with, "That's not true. I was on time in April." Her focus is now on defending herself and proving you wrong.

One important goal for you to promote is cooperation and teamwork. Using words like *we, our,* and *us* conveys the message that the objective is mutual and that achieving it is in the best interest of you both. Read the following scenario and outcomes for additional ways to apply your language skills.

SCENARIO

You have a mentor who is coming in once a week to observe you and your child care curriculum. The last time she arrived, she received numerous phone calls and talked loudly on her cell phone. You and the children found it disruptive and distracting.

Option 1: You say, "You are distracting the children. You need to turn off your cell phone in my child care!"

Outcome 1: People do not react well to demands. The mentor is likely to become defensive.

Option 2: You say, "We need to have your cell phone turned off in my child care!"

Outcome 2: Even though you used the word *we* in this situation, the mentor might still perceive the statement as a demand. As a result, she is likely to become defensive.

Option 3: You say, "The children are easily distracted when you get a phone call. Why don't you use the next room so you can take your call in quiet?"

Outcome 3: Here you are stating the problem and sharing in the solution without criticizing the person. You are focusing on the action that must be taken and not the person.

In the case study, if Simone had been more assertive, the outcome might not have been quite so negative. For example, Simone could have prepared a small flyer that asks everyone to use the child care door. When Kara came to the front door, Simone could have let her in and asked her to wipe her feet carefully. In a relaxed manner, she could then have said, "I know it is important that *we* conduct the visit, but I really need you to respect my wishes and use the child care door in the future." Simone could then give her the flyer to help her remember at the next visit.

Walking the fine line between assertive and aggressive behavior can be difficult. A parent who knows she owes you paperwork and has forgotten it again might anticipate your reaction and behave defensively. She could over-react, confronting you aggressively and emotionally before you are prepared for it. When a parent or monitor acts aggressively, do not take it personally. Remember that she is probably angry at the situation, not at you.

CHALLENGE: Understanding Others' Points of View

Part of being assertive is listening well to other people. Let them know that you want to understand their point of view. *Remember: understanding is different from agreeing.* You can understand what someone is saying and still disagree with her. This type of assertive listening takes dedication and practice.

SOLUTION: Show That You Value What Others Say

Have you ever had a discussion with someone who was obviously not paying attention to what you were saying? It's frustrating to feel that the person you are talking to does not value what you have to say. If you use assertive listening skills, you will never make a person feel this way. You will listen, *really* listen, to what she is saying. Here's how:

1. **Concentrate.** This type of listening begins with concentration. Often in a stressful or emotionally charged situation, you can find it hard to concentrate because your thoughts are racing.

2. **Relax.** Try to gain your composure and relax. This is not always easy; you might need to excuse yourself and go to another room until you feel ready to concentrate.

3. **Check your body language.** When you listen, remember how important body language can be. If you are tense, tapping your foot, or sitting rigidly, the other person might start to mirror your body language. Try to sit or stand in a relaxed way. Lean toward her, keeping your body open and relaxed, showing that you are listening. Occasionally nod your head. Displaying an open posture encourages the person to speak.

4. **Ask questions.** After listening, tell the person what you have understood her to say. If she does not agree, ask questions. Encourage her to voice her thoughts, opinions, and feelings. If you still do not understand her point of view, tell her you are confused and ask her to clarify. Continue to tell her that you might be coming from a different perspective, but you are interested in her thoughts on the situation.

5. **Establish mutual respect.** When you validate a person's response respectfully, she might be more receptive to hearing your point of view. Establishing this level of mutual respect will be helpful throughout your relationship.

CHALLENGE: Trying to Predict How Interactions Might Go

When you anticipate that an upcoming conversation might be difficult, good preparation includes knowing what you want to accomplish. However, you cannot know for sure how the other person will react to your objective, so you must be prepared for a variety of outcomes and perspectives.

SOLUTION: Focus on Your Intended Outcomes

Prepare your responses to the reactions you can anticipate. Think about mutual goals for yourself and the other person. Practice how to present those goals. In the case study, rather that greeting Kara with folded arms and a negative attitude, Simone would have benefited from having a mutual goal—to complete the visit successfully—rather than dwelling on her desire to make Kara use the child care door. Your preparation should include examining your past history with the person you are going to confront. Ask yourself questions like these:

- Are you ever out of compliance when this person visits?

- Does this parent try to make you responsible for the solution?

- Do you often have confrontations with visitors?

  - How do you handle parents who forget diapers, paperwork, or other requests?

- How do you respond to regulators who are always late, ignore your requests, or otherwise behave passive-aggressively?
- Do you identify mutual goals for yourself and the other person?

Asking and answering these questions can help you develop your strategy for addressing problems. Think about mutually beneficial outcomes. In Simone and Kara's case, both needed to complete a visit. Simone could have thought about her attitude, concentrated on the goal, and decided how to handle the situation differently.

SOLUTION: Use Documentation to Your Advantage

It is important that you document all your efforts and requests for information. If you are considering suspending a child because the parent does not bring you the required paperwork, document how many times you have requested it and how you requested it (written, verbal, phone call). Have documentation to show the parent that you must adhere to the regulation. By showing the regulation or requirement in writing, you are backing up your request. If your problem is with a regulator, document what the problem is and what steps you have taken to solve the problem.

Have you ever heard, "But I didn't know you wanted me to . . . ?" Occasionally, misunderstandings can occur. Your concern or request may have been misinterpreted, or the person may not have realized the importance of your request. For example, a parent might say, "I didn't know you needed the paperwork *this week*." Be aware, however, that this could just be an excuse for not taking care of your request. Therefore, document the day, time, outcome, expected action, time frame, and any other additional information about your attempts to correct a situation. In some situations, when an agreement is reached, the written agreement should be signed and a copy given to both parties. This document can be used to minimize future misunderstandings.

CHALLENGE: Maintaining an Appropriate Balance of Authority

Maintaining a balance of authority while keeping a positive attitude is not always easy. You are faced with many conflicting views of who should be in charge. Your clients might feel they are in charge because you are caring for their children. They might feel they have the authority to tell you how they want their children cared for. They might not take your requests seriously. Parents sometimes feel that because they are paying for your child care services, they should have the authority to make certain demands. Examples of conflicts in balancing your authority with that of parents include dealing with a parent who

- does not want a child to nap and expects you to rearrange your schedule;
- tells you that she wants you to let a child watch a TV program that you find disruptive to other children in your child care; and
- brings sugary donuts or cookies for a child and tells you to give this food to the child instead of the breakfast the other children are eating.

Similarly, visitors who are at your home for the purpose of mandatory inspections, licensing, monitoring, mentoring, evaluations, and observing might feel they are in charge because their visits are mandatory and they can impose consequences for noncompliance. Examples of conflicts in balancing your authority with that of regulators include dealing with a regulator who

- feels she has the right to go into any room in your home;
- tells you to rearrange your child care space;
- is not respectful of your role as a business owner; and
- does not respect your right to privacy.

SOLUTION: Stand Up for Yourself

These are just a few examples of ways that others may try to extend their authority beyond the scope of their statutory rights. As a family child care provider, you must comply with your responsibilities and regulations affecting the children, parents, and visitors of your child care. However, there are circumstances when you must assert your own authority over your business. Here are two examples:

A parent wants you to change your schedule or allow activities that conflict with your philosophy to accommodate his child. You have the authority to develop a schedule that is age appropriate and fits your philosophy for all the children. If making changes disrupts the other children, you have the right to refuse his request. Your philosophy may stress nonviolence and peaceful resolutions. What may be acceptable in the child's home is not necessarily acceptable in your child care. For example, watching a violent cartoon in the morning might trigger inappropriate behaviors in some children. You set the rules and standards in your child care. Make sure that parents are given a copy of your policies before their children start in your program. Do not make exceptions. For example, if your rule is that children cannot bring toy guns or weapons and a parent overrides that rule, you need to develop the assertiveness skills to enforce your rule. These skills will help you deal with clients who do not pay on time, are always late, bring inappropriate food or toys, or continually forget diapers, paperwork, and other requests.

A licensor tells you she wants you to move your license from one wall to another because she thinks it is more prominent on the other wall. You have authority over how you set up your environment. As long as the arrangement is safe and age appropriate, you can decide the most convenient places for your equipment and documentation, including where you display your license.

When a licensor or other regulator requires you to make a change that you feel is beyond her scope of authority, ask to see the regulation that requires you to make the change. If a visitor asks you to do something you are uncomfortable with, such as leaving the children unattended to go to another room to get paperwork, you have the authority to speak up and say you cannot do that because of regulations. Using the skills discussed in this chapter can help you to become more comfortable exercising your authority and negotiating for positive outcomes.

CASE STUDY 2:
Simone Plans to Accomplish Goals and Prevent Disasters

A few months ago, when Kara came for her visit, Simone asked her to please use the child care door in the back for future visits. Kara just brushed off the request, saying, "Oh, yeah, if I remember." Simone felt that Kara had not taken her seriously. As the next month approached, Simone began to wonder if Kara would comply with her wishes and use the back door.

Simone loves her child care business and the children she cares for. She acknowledges that Kara did have the authority to come to her home once a month, but she also realizes that she has the authority to request which door visitors use. She is determined that she is not going to let Kara overstep her boundaries.

This is hard for Simone. She understands that she is a passive person by nature. Recently, Simone attended an assertiveness training workshop, and she wants to put her new skills into practice. She remembers that preparation is an important part of being assertive. She begins to plan how she will handle Kara's next visit. If Kara goes to the child care door in back, Simone will thank her and there will be no issue. As part of her preparation, she also thinks about what her response will be if Kara goes to the front door and how it will affect the outcome.

Simone's first thought is to refuse to let Kara in the front door and ask her to go around to the back. This course of action would certainly lead to a confrontation, and Simone wants to avoid this outcome.

The second course of action is to let Kara in, but Simone wonders if this would be giving in and letting Kara win. Then she remembers that this should not be a win-lose but a win-win situation. She thinks about their mutual goal: the mandatory visit must be conducted. Simone is going to accept this challenge and see if she can turn this situation into a collaboration instead of a confrontation.

Simone is going to give Kara the benefit of the doubt and accept her explanation that she forgot Simone's request to go to the back door. Simone takes the small sign that asks all visitors to use the back child care door and places it above the doorbell. She then prints out a letter explaining the change and asking all visitors to use the back door. The letter is written to all visitors and does not single out Kara. These reminders may help Kara and eliminate her "I forgot" excuse.

Simone's third plan is to let Kara in without becoming angry and to try to remain respectful while Kara conducts her visit. Afterward, she will ask Kara to sit down with her for a few minutes, and she will use good eye contact and a respectful tone of voice to tell Kara to please use the back door. She will also give Kara the printed letter. If Kara gets angry or tries to brush her off, Simone will listen to what Kara is saying and let her know she understands or ask questions if Kara does not understand, but she will remain firm in her request.

Simone decides she can say, "I know *we* both need to have this visit conducted. So next month when you come to the back door, I will have my records right at the door so *we* can get *our* visit done quickly and efficiently."

Simone knows that Kara is not the easiest person to deal with, but she feels prepared for any outcome. She hopes her positive attitude can create a mutual respect that makes the visits more successful.

Checkpoints for Success

Think about the last confrontation you had with a client or regulator. Use the following checklist to help you identify your strengths and weaknesses during the confrontation. Doing so offers you an opportunity to think about what you could have done differently.

___ I felt comfortable using my assertiveness skills.

___ I was able to negotiate a solution to the problem and felt comfortable with the resolution.

___ I used assertive language effectively.

___ I gave constructive feedback.

___ I understood the other person's point of view and let the person know that I understood.

___ I documented any agreements or the outcome.

PARTICIPATE FULLY IN VISITS

Family child care providers are busy. Your ability to multitask while maintaining a positive attitude and a high energy level is very important. These are essential qualities during the day-to-day operations of your business and when you are participating in a visit.

CASE STUDY 1:
Karen and John Distractedly Receive Visitors

Karen has been successfully providing child care for a few years. Karen's husband, John, has decided to join her in operating the business. This is an exciting as well as an important decision for their family. In the state where they live, having another adult present offers Karen an opportunity to increase her program's enrollment. This is important because increased enrollment means Karen and John can both work from their home.

To accommodate the increased enrollment, Karen and John have converted their garage into a child care room. The conversion has not only represented a considerable financial investment but also a large investment of time and labor—they have done a great deal of the work themselves. To use their newly renovated space, they must receive approval from the local building inspector and their licensor.

During construction, Karen has continued to operate her program in her existing licensed space. On the day of the scheduled inspections, Karen and John are present, along with six children under the age of five. According to plan, they are organizing a game in the outside play area when the building inspector arrives. Much to their surprise, he not only wants to view the new construction but expresses a desire to inspect the entire house.

Their original plan was that Karen would stay outside and supervise the children, leaving John to accompany the inspector. Just as Karen is getting the children settled, however, her licensor arrives. Unfortunately for Karen, her licensor is in the neighborhood and has decided to come by a little earlier than originally scheduled. As a result of this early arrival, Karen must gather the children and bring them inside so she can accompany the licensor during her inspection. The children are not happy about having their outside playtime end so abruptly.

As Karen attempts to organize her group and go inside, two of the younger children begin to cry. Karen has also caught a glimpse of John following the building inspector through their home, and things do not appear to be going well. To make matters worse, Karen's licensor has been talking nonstop since they entered the house. Karen knows she should be paying closer attention, but the children are upset and not cooperating, and she is concerned about what is happening with John.

John is distracted as well. He knows the licensor has arrived earlier than expected, and he can hear children crying. The original plan was for the building inspector to have completed his visit by the time the licensor arrived. This would have allowed John to stay with the children while Karen gave her undivided attention to the licensing inspection. John is wondering how Karen is doing while he attempts to answer all the building inspector's questions.

John is also worried that Karen might not remember the questions she needs to ask the licensor about when they can accept new children. They have already interviewed families and have children they will lose if they can't quickly enroll them. John is trying to pay close attention to the building inspector, but he is beginning to have a problem understanding exactly what needs to be done. John wonders if the inspector is simply making recommendations or is saying that everything he has mentioned needs to be changed prior to approving the addition.

Ninety minutes later, John and Karen are finally able to talk with each other. What happened? Neither of them heard or understood everything communicated to them. The building inspector has left a written list, but John can't read his writing. He is still unsure what changes are actually required prior to approval. Karen is concerned that she didn't ask all the necessary questions. She is also concerned because now she has to wait for her licensor to send her a report. At this point, Karen has no idea how long that will take or what the report will contain. The sad truth is that Karen and John are no better informed now than they were before their inspection visits took place.

CHALLENGE: Making Visits an Interactive Process

In the case study, the needs of both the inspector and the licensor were met as soon as they completed their required inspection visits. However, it's clear that the needs of Karen and John were not met. What could Karen and John have done differently to ensure that their needs were also met during this process?

Success during visits like these begins with a positive attitude and good planning. If you are a provider who looks at a visit the same way you look at a trip to the dentist—as something being done to you, with the potential for being both costly and painful—you underestimate your role as a provider and business owner. A visit should be interactive. This means that all involved should share the expectation of having their needs met. If you expect to feel any satisfaction at the conclusion of a visit or an inspection, you need to have been an actual participant (not simply an onlooker) in the process.

So the question becomes: How do you become a positive participant in this process?

SOLUTION: Document What Happens

One important way in which you can ensure your active participation is to start using documentation to your advantage. Why document? Karen and John's case provides a clear answer. Because Karen and John did not take notes, they were left in a state of confusion. They had only the handwritten list from the building inspector, and neither of them could read it.

Imagine how much better the couple would have felt if they had their own written records of what was said and what occurred. If they had asked the right questions and had documented carefully, they would have known exactly what they still needed to do to expand the business. They would probably have had an approximate time frame for approval. This would have allowed them to give specific information to the families waiting to hear about a starting date.

Begin the documentation process by establishing your objectives before any visit takes place. If you have requested an inspection or a regulator has scheduled a visit, use this advance notice as an opportunity to determine exactly what you want to get out of the visit. To prepare for unscheduled visits, keep a running written list that you can refer to when a visitor drops by unannounced. When you make a written list, you are providing yourself with a visual reminder that you can refer to throughout the visit. The following is an example:

> Obtain information on local trainings.
>
> Ask about the new regulation for napping infants.
>
> Ask about the outside fencing (new height requirement?).
>
> Ask for new menus and attendance forms.

If Karen and John had created lists that clearly outlined their objectives, John might have been better able to obtain the specific information he needed to get their renovated space approved as quickly as possible. Karen would not have forgotten what she wanted to ask the licensor. They also would have found it easier to stay focused despite distractions.

SOLUTION: Control the Tempo of the Visit

Often during a visit, the person visiting you uses a data collection tool. This means a lot of the information collected is in checklist form. Doing this allows the visitor to walk through your home and talk while checking off observations. This process usually works well for the visitors. It allows them to multitask and to use their time as efficiently as possible. It also allows for a quicker visit. Most people do not want to make a visit last any longer than necessary. If the tempo of the visit does not allow your needs to be met, however, you need to be prepared to take some control. One of the ways you can do this is by introducing your own data collection tool.

How well this would have worked for Karen! Karen's licensor arrived earlier than scheduled, and this created a problem. Karen would have been well within her rights to request that the licensor return at the scheduled time. If that was not practical, Karen could have suggested that the licensor not begin the inspection until Karen was able to organize her group and get them involved in an activity. Karen could have informed her licensor that she needed time to prepare to take notes as well as retrieve her own checklist. In doing this, Karen could have retained some control over the timing and tempo of the visit. This would have resulted in a more interactive and satisfactory experience.

If John had carried a notepad and had been prepared to take notes, he probably would have stopped the building inspector periodically to write down the specific information he needed. Statements such as, "Let me see if I understand exactly what you are saying" or "Let me read my list back to you to make sure we are on the same page" are examples of effective interactive strategies. By taking notes, John could have slowed down the process and made it less confusing. When the visit ended, John could have had his own written record of what occurred, and he would not have had to rely solely on the inspector's unreadable list.

SOLUTION: Achieve a Balance of Authority during Your Professional Interactions

Usually one of the primary objectives of a visit is to evaluate the accountability of you and your program. Are you accountable for what you have agreed to in regulations and contracts? Is your program accountable for the needs of the children who participate? By taking good notes during a visit, you place yourself in a position where you, too, can evaluate accountability.

In order to operate your program properly, you depend on the accuracy of the information you are given. Often when people recognize a written record is being made of their statements, they are more thoughtful before speaking. For example, they are more likely to clearly differentiate between their opinions and what is actually required by regulation. When you take the time to document what is said during the visit, you can respectfully call attention to any apparent differences between what you are told and what you believe your regulations and/or contracts state. Professionals should be able to hold one another accountable.

Keeping a written record of all the monitoring visits conducted in your home can be an invaluable way to protect your professional reputation. For example, many states now post licensing histories on their official state websites. If you believe the information posted about your program on your state's website is incorrect or incomplete, your documentation can assist you in correcting any false or misleading information.

In some states, providers are required to keep a folder of all the information sent to them by their regulatory authority, including citations. You are then required to make this information available to any parent who wants to review it. In most states, if families call the regulatory authority to check on your background, they are given all your pertinent information—including any citations you may have received as part of your licensing history.

Think how much easier it would be when explaining citations or challenging citations to refer to your own comprehensive notes. This would allow you to give an accurate account of events, regardless of how much time has elapsed. This in no way implies that you can ignore or negate legitimate citations, but it does allow you to explain in your own words what you believe occurred. It also provides you with the opportunity to explain how, when necessary, you corrected any issues that were brought to your attention.

CHALLENGE: Remaining Focused throughout a Visit

Usually a lot of distractions are present in a typical family child care environment. It's true that you seldom have two inspections occurring at the same time, but often there are more than enough distractions to go around.

SOLUTION: Concentrate on Taking Notes

Just as regulators can stay better focused by using checklists, you, too, can stay better focused by taking good notes during a visit.

For your notes to be accurate, you should write them down while events are unfolding. Whenever possible, do not try to recreate events after the fact. Here are some tips to help you take notes effectively:

- Always date your notes and include the time of the visit.
- Include the names of all the adults present and the names and ages of any children present.
- Write legibly. If you use a type of shorthand, make sure you can easily understand what you have written.
- State the purpose of the visit (examples: simple monitoring, mentoring visit, food program visit, complaint investigation).
- Do not include personal comments or opinions in your notes unless you feel they have bearing on the business and outcome of the visit. If you feel the person visiting you is behaving inappropriately, for example, you need to give specific examples of what was said or done that made you come to that conclusion.
- If you asked questions, include each question as well as the answer in your notes.
- Try not to exaggerate or distort events. For your notes to be credible, they should be as accurate and as factual as possible.

Many regulators use data collection tools that require your signature at the conclusion of the visit. Read what has been presented to you carefully before you sign. If you disagree with it, ask if you can make a rebuttal note on the document. If this is not allowed, make sure you include that fact, as well as your rebuttal notes, in your own written record. Do not sign anything that misrepresents your interpretation of events.

Request that your regulator read, initial, and date your visit notes prior to leaving your home. This helps both you and the regulator avoid any future misunderstandings about what was actually recorded during the visit. Don't feel pressured. Take a deep breath and take the time to document accurately.

Your notes do not have to be extensive, but at the very least they should include whatever is not reflected or differs from what is included in the visitor's checklist. Keeping your own visit notes allows you to have something in writing that reflects what you heard and observed during the visit. This might provide you with some protection if the visit report you receive in the mail contains information that you think differs substantially from what was discussed or occurred.

In the case of visits that do not include monitoring tools or the use of checklists (mentoring or early intervention visits, for example), make sure you are documenting all the important points communicated during the visit. Ask yourself, "What information do I need to have in my possession after this person leaves my home?"

SOLUTION: Prepare Children in Advance for Visitors

Just as you practice fire drills and emergency evacuation plans, you can and should practice scenarios that help children understand what they can and should do when someone visits your child care setting, including unannounced visits. It's amazing how even the youngest child, with sufficient practice, can successfully participate in an emergency evacuation. The same is equally true of young children who have been prepared for a visitor to their child care setting.

For example, you could develop a plan that includes creating a "Visit Box" with special puzzles, which the children know has been set aside for when visitors arrive. Talk to the children about the adults who may visit, as well as why they visit your program.

Make sure that whatever your plan includes, you can see and hear the children at all times. If a child is in distress or needs your attention, don't be hesitant to ask the visitor to halt the visit long enough for you to attend to his needs.

CASE STUDY 2:
Karen and John Concentrate on Inspector Visits

Karen has been providing child care for a few years. Karen's husband, John, has decided to join her in the operation of the business. Karen and John have discussed this at length and have investigated all the financial ramifications this type of partnership would entail. After serious consideration, they have decided to move forward with their plan.

Because an additional full-time adult allows Karen and John to care for more children, they have converted their garage to a large child care room. Before they invested the time and money in this conversion, Karen and John did their homework. They know what type of inspections they need, and they also know exactly what the inspections will involve.

Karen and John have scheduled the building inspection and the licensing inspection for the same day but at different times. Because Karen has practiced her "Visit Plan" with the children, they are prepared to work on puzzles and other games during the inspection visits.

When the building inspector arrives and asks to inspect the entire house, John is prepared. John politely tells the inspector he will be happy to receive feedback on the overall condition of the house but adds that he did ask for the scope of the inspection when he scheduled the appointment. Continuing to speak courteously, John informs the building inspector that he was told the scope of this inspection would include only the conversion. The building inspector agrees to begin his inspection with the new addition. John has a list of questions he prepared prior to the visit, and Karen is taking notes. At the conclusion of the inspection, Karen and John have had all their questions answered. They also have a written list that clearly differentiates between recommendations and what is required before their addition can be approved. Finally, they have a time line they can share with the parents on their waiting list.

Karen's licensor arrives earlier than expected, while the building inspector is still in their home. Karen politely informs her that she is involved in another inspection. She gives the licensor the option of leaving and returning at the scheduled time or waiting until the building inspection is complete. Karen's licensor opts to leave and return later.

When the licensor returns at the scheduled time, John and Karen are waiting and prepared to accompany her during the licensing inspection. Karen has a list of prepared questions, and John takes notes. At the conclusion of the visit, Karen and John understand what remains to be done and have a time frame for approval.

This has been a very productive day! Both visits have been successfully concluded, and Karen and John feel satisfaction in knowing exactly where they stand and how soon they can expand their business.

Checkpoints for Success

___ I have conducted regular practice sessions with the children in my program to help prepare them for visitors.

___ I have kept an ongoing and accessible list of questions or requests for information and resources for use during unexpected visits.

___ I have accessible materials (pen and paper or laptop, checklists, questions I want answered) to use when creating my own visit record.

___ I create visit notes that are legible and accurate.

___ I ask each regulator to date and initial notes before leaving my home.

___ I file my visit notes after a visit as quickly as possible so they do not get misplaced or lost.

FOLLOW-UP

It's tempting to ignore or put off dealing with something that seems inconvenient or unpleasant. Unfortunately, ignoring things does not make them go away. As a matter of fact, the result is often quite the opposite: things you could have taken care of comparatively easily frequently become much larger problems when not addressed in a timely fashion.

CASE STUDY 1:
Kay's Confidence Is Uninformed

Kay has been providing child care in her home for twenty-eight years. During this time, she has worked hard and has established a good reputation in her community. Not only does Kay always have a waiting list; she has also earned the respect of her peers. She has been a mentor and has sat on state-sponsored committees to examine regulations. She has applied for and earned national accreditation. Kay has always felt a great confidence in her ability to operate a successful family child care business.

Over the years, Kay has seen many regulators come and go. When she first became licensed, she was very nervous about the periodic inspections necessary to maintain her license and enrollment in the food program. Eventually, Kay realized that she often seemed better informed about the requirements for operating her business than many of the people visiting her home. On many occasions, she found herself instructing her regulators. Kay also found that because of staff turnover, few of the same individuals actually came back a second time. As a result, she found herself half listening to what they had to say.

In short, Kay feels she knows best. Although she nods her head in agreement, she rarely makes any changes as a result of what a regulator says. Because of the turnover of staff visiting her home, Kay feels comfortable ignoring anything sent to her as the result of a visit. It is not uncommon for Kay to discard envelopes without even opening them. Based on her experience, the chances are quite good she will never see the person who initiated the report a second time.

Recently, Kay's state decided to post its child care providers' licensing information on its public website. The decision was made to help prospective clients view each child care provider's licensing history. When this was proposed as a new initiative, Kay was one of its biggest supporters. She wanted the people in her community to recognize the difference between good programs and not so good programs. Kay is confident about her position because she is absolutely certain she operates a very good program.

On the first day the posting appears, Kay immediately goes to the site and looks for her information. Much to her embarrassment, Kay finds something she has not anticipated: twenty years' worth of citations posted and visible for the whole world to see. Although most of the citations are not serious, the cumulative effect of so many citations is likely to be disastrous. How could this have happened? What should she do?

CHALLENGE: Responding to Issues When They Are Raised

Although you are a small business owner caring for children in your home, you are also a professional who is operating a business. Not only is it your job to understand relevant regulations, contracts, and laws, but you are also responsible for responding when necessary to the professionals who conduct visits in your home. One of the most frequent causes of legal action taken against family child care programs is providers who do not respond appropriately to citations.

SOLUTION: Take Every Communication Seriously

Because continuity of care is one of the benchmarks of quality family child care, longevity in your profession should be a great testimony to your success. In reality, however, anyone in the child care business who assumes her experience or standing in the community offers her immunity when it comes to operating by the rules is not thinking correctly. The scrutiny directed at early childhood programs cannot be avoided. Even if you never see the same regulator twice, each one has authority, and it is your responsibility to stay in regulatory compliance. If you take the position that you can ignore issues raised during a visit, simply throw away a letter or report unopened, or never choose to deal with the consequences of those actions, you are not acting in your own best interest. When you choose not to hear the message or simply choose to ignore anything you do not agree with, the data from the visits does not simply go away.

As Kay sadly discovered, the fact that she was allowed to continue to operate her business did not mean she didn't have a substantial history of citations. In fact, she had a citation history that could easily cause families reviewing Kay's online information to think long and hard before enrolling a child. Kay's initial reaction when reading the information posted on the site was surprise. She wondered where this information came from and why she hadn't been made aware of it before it was posted.

After recovering from her surprise, Kay felt angry and blamed the agency or the individuals she believed were responsible. Why had they blindsided her? Why hadn't someone contacted her to talk about the noncompliances posted under her name? She could have told them that many of the citations had been corrected at the time of the visit or shortly thereafter. She would have been happy to clarify information that was misleading or incorrect.

Unfortunately, Kay was informed about the noncompliances. She simply chose not to hear what was said to her at the time of her visits and chose not to read the resulting paperwork. Based on her experience, Kay believed that no substantial consequence existed to ignoring what she didn't agree with or what she found inconvenient to address. She was a great believer in no news is good news. Kay was unable to tell the difference between no news and ignored news.

SOLUTION: Regularly Check on Your Status

Posting licensing information on the Internet is becoming common throughout the United States. If this is occurring in your state and you are only now determining your licensing status by referring to a website, you have placed yourself and your program at a disadvantage. A proactive provider makes it her business to know all the information appearing next to her name long before it is posted. As Kay discovered, a list of cited noncompliances listed on a public website, no matter how inconsequential she believes each individual citation is, often has an adverse effect on people using the site to obtain information about your program.

A successful child care business is especially reliant on a credible reputation. Parents enrolling children in your program want assurance that you are operating in an appropriate manner. To you, one electrical receptacle without a cover or insert may not seem like such a big deal in the overall scheme of things. To prospective clients, however, the fact that you're operating a child care business and have not taken the precaution of checking all your receptacles might make the difference in whether they decide to enroll their child.

In the case study, Kay benefited from referrals by peers throughout her career. But now that other professionals can read her long list of noncompliances, they are likely to think twice before recommending her. Kay's ability to mentor is likely to be challenged after a review of her posted licensing history. Although some of the information contained on the site may be misleading or incorrect, Kay will have a difficult time making the case that the process has been unfair. She is the one who chose to disregard important information when it was made available to her.

You need to be aware that, for the most part, information obtained during a visit is public. Even if you live in a state that does not currently post licensing information online, you can reasonably assume that a parent calling your regulatory authority receives all of your pertinent licensing history, including citations. Prospective clients are often given information about the duration of your license, your quota, any adult household members, and any citations. A growing number of parents seek out licensed or registered providers specifically so they can receive this type of information. You should also know that information about your business is shared among the agencies that send representatives to visit your program. If you are being sanctioned or terminated by your food program, for example, it is highly probable that your licensing authority is aware of the problem.

CHALLENGE: Deciding What to Own

That old saying "To err is human" is worth remembering. Everyone makes mistakes, and no one always makes the right decisions. If you are completely honest with yourself, you admit that spending your time acknowledging your mistakes and correcting them is a lot more productive than attempting to always justify yourself or demonize the person who "caught" you.

When you are working hard and focusing on the well-being of children, having someone come into your home and point out what he believes you are doing wrong is difficult to take. You might feel that the process is especially unfair when you find yourself in noncompliance as the direct result of accommodations you make to the needs of the families of children in your care. It isn't hard to sympathize with someone in Kay's situation, who often did know more about the operation of her business than some of the people paid to evaluate her program.

SOLUTION: Take the Lessons You Teach Children to Heart

Remember that in your role as a family child care provider, you often find yourself instructing children about doing things correctly. To establish a sense of security for all the children in your program, you create rules that govern their behavior and provide a framework for your daily routine. If you are good at what you do, you recognize that when children make mistakes, you have an important opportunity to teach. It's also true that adults benefit from acknowledging their mistakes and correcting them.

If your licensor, monitor, or inspector finds you are not in compliance during a visit and you know you are not in compliance, your most effective actions are to own it, correct it, and get past it. You might feel there are extenuating circumstances, and you are perfectly free to explain what they are and how they affected your decision. Remember, though, that your explanation should not disregard or attempt to justify an obvious noncompliance. If it does, you may place yourself in a position that makes you appear unwilling or unable to correct problems. That, in turn, can raise larger questions about your overall ability to provide appropriate child care. You may not agree with all the regulations pertaining to your business, but disagreeing does not mean you can pick and choose what you will and will not comply with.

Chapter 6 discusses the importance of documentation and your right to question citations. You should question decisions that you feel are incorrect. However, there is a distinct difference between challenging a citation and attempting to justify an obvious noncompliance. For example, take the case of overenrollment. You might have been overenrolled on the day of a visit because you were helping out a parent. You might feel strongly that you did the right thing and that, given the same set of circumstances, you would do it again. If that is the case, you need to understand the possible consequences of your decision. Regulations governing quota were established to protect the health and safety of all enrolled children.

In your role as a responsible business owner, you need to acknowledge any noncompliance and find ways to avoid the same compliance issue in the future. If you feel the regulations in your state are unreasonable, you need to identify appropriate forums where you can give feedback and work for change. Ignoring or disregarding a regulation is not realistic. Just as you teach children the rules and assist them in understanding how rules allow everyone to participate in a safe and meaningful way, so you should demonstrate your understanding of this principle by complying with your family child care regulations.

CHALLENGE: Understanding Regulations and Citations

Before you respond to citations, you must make sure you know what you're talking about. Chapter 3 discusses how good preparation works in your favor. Staying informed means keeping current with any changes to your regulations or contractual information. This can be challenging because regulatory language can be confusing and open to interpretation. When a citation does occur, it is frequently because of a misinterpretation or a false assumption about a regulation.

One regulation that is often open to interpretation is the direct supervision regulation. In most states, direct supervision of children is required at all times. This appears to be very straightforward, but the reality of caring for multiage children often is complex and challenging. What does direct supervision really mean? If you work alone and are licensed to care for six children, when you need to use the bathroom, are you required to bring them all in with you? What should happen at naptime? Does direct supervision mean you need to sit directly next to mats or cribs the entire time children are sleeping? What about outdoor play—can you legally sit on a deck to supervise older children who are outside playing while listening through an open door to supervise younger children napping inside? What about when you are preparing lunch—if children are in an adjacent room and you can hear and have immediate access to them, is that sufficient? Just how can you get questions like these reliably answered?

SOLUTION: Be Persistent until You Have Clarification

Agencies usually create policies to clarify certain, if not all, regulations. You should ask the visitor about the availability of these policies, and when copies are available, request one. If a policy or clarification is not available, you need to create your own reference by asking specific questions. For example, if you ask your licensor if direct supervision means you need to take all of the child care children into the bathroom with you, and your licensor replies, "Of course not!" get her response in writing. If the visitor is unwilling to put her response in writing, include her response in your visit notes, and have her date and sign them before leaving your home.

You can also request that the visitor provide you with acceptable options describing how to meet the intent of your state's direct supervision regulation. Ask specific questions and use specific scenarios, such as the ones included here. Make sure you record whatever she tells you, and have her date and sign notes.

This might seem like a lot of additional responsibility for you, but if you do decide to challenge a citation, you should have as much documentation as possible to support your position. This is also important when it comes to issues about your liability. Unfortunately, children do get hurt in child care. Often when this occurs, your supervision (or lack thereof) becomes the focal point of any subsequent investigation. If you have implemented procedures that you believe meet the intent of regulations, you should have something in writing that protects you.

Never assume anything. In a majority of states, your profession is strictly regulated. Yet one of the most common complaints we hear from providers is about the lack of consistency in interpreting or applying regulations. This is an area that leaves providers feeling at their most vulnerable. If you are about to be cited for noncompliance during a visit, you should always ask to see the pertinent regulation. If the visitor does not have a copy of the regulations, produce yours.

Once you review the regulation, if you still feel it does not apply specifically to your situation, ask if the visitor is using something other than the regulation (for example, a policy or an internal memo) to justify the citation.

If that turns out not to be the case, politely ask the visitor to explain the specific rationale for the citation. Make sure you take notes. If you are asking appropriate questions and taking good notes, you will be prepared and better able to formally respond if and when you do receive the citation.

CHALLENGE: Responding to Citations and/or Legal Orders Appropriately

One of the ways you demonstrate your professionalism is how you respond to citations. The very nature of family child care can make it especially difficult for regulators and providers to interact in a totally objective manner. Although you are operating a business in your home, it is still your home. If a regulator cites your environment for poor sanitation, for example, her criticism can be very hard to hear. Regulators are sometimes overly sensitive as well and may omit their observation while speaking to you but then include their citation in a follow-up report.

Issues like sanitation can also fall into the gray area of interpretation and subjective evaluation. Unfortunately, what is an unsanitary environment to one visitor might appear as nothing more than the appropriate clutter of child care to another. Because of this, you should try not to take evaluations or assessments personally. That is easier said than done, but remember: if your goal is to continue operating your business, you need to find a reasonable and unemotional way to deal with citations. Becoming angry, attempting to retaliate, or choosing to ignore citations only makes you look unprofessional. Such responses can also lead to the suspension of your license or registration.

SOLUTION: Give a Rebuttal or Make Corrections Immediately

So what actions should you take upon receiving a citation? First and foremost, carefully read any information you receive from your regulator and/or the agencies that send representatives to evaluate your program. If the visitor hands you a report before leaving your home, read it carefully and do not sign it if you do not agree, unless you can include your rebuttal along with your signature.

If you do sign a report that you believe contains incorrect information without including your rebuttal, in effect you are acknowledging that you agree with all of the information. Don't feel compelled to sign anything if you feel it does not accurately reflect what occurred during the visit. Remember: your rebuttal should not be an excuse or justification for something you know is a violation. Instead, it is your explanation of why you believe you are not in violation.

Make sure any noncompliance you have corrected during the visit (locking a gate, inserting an outlet cover, posting your evacuation route) is reflected in the report. The more quickly a noncompliance is corrected, the better. If you can, correct whatever is brought to your attention immediately. In some cases, if a compliance issue can be dealt with during a visit, it will not be included in the overall assessment. If the citation is omitted, that is all well and good, but if it is not, having the correction included in the report is to your advantage.

If the report contains citations based on a subjective evaluation, you should request that the visitor give specific examples of how she came to her conclusions. For example, if the report states that your "food preparation area is unsanitary," it is the visitor's responsibility to substantiate that claim. Is it because the counter surface was sticky? Were there crumbs? How did she make her determination? If you feel her assessment is incorrect, you can respond more effectively once you know exactly how she reached her conclusion.

If you do not receive a copy of the report at the conclusion of the visit but instead receive it in the mail, read it carefully and immediately. Procrastination will not change what the report contains. Make sure you compare the information in the report with the notes you took during the visit. Remember to check carefully for any discrepancies.

SOLUTION: Pay Attention to Deadlines

Keep in mind that important time lines are usually included in citation or deficiency reports. You are commonly given a specific date by which you must respond. You should also be given a specific time line for the correction of any noncompliances. If you receive a legal order as a result of a visit, such as a cease and desist order, a time limit is usually given for your appeal. It is in your best interest to read and respond to any report sent to you as quickly as possible. Do not make the mistake of thinking you can be unresponsive—not if you want to continue operating your business! Your timely response not only demonstrates your professionalism, but it also gives you an opportunity to tell your side of the story. In some states, once an agency has received your response about the correction of any noncompliance, the corresponding citations are removed from your licensing history. Find out what the policy is in your state.

Never state that you have corrected a noncompliance unless you have actually done so. Usually, when legal action is taken against a provider by a regulatory authority or a food program sponsor, it is because of cumulative problems. If a violation has been brought to your attention and you lie about correcting it, or you are made aware of the same violation repeatedly and you do nothing to address the problem, you leave yourself and your business in a very vulnerable position. If you do receive a legal order as a result of a serious noncompliance (the death or serious injury of a child, fraud, or a noncompliance that has repeatedly been brought to your attention without correction), it might be advisable for you to seek advice from an attorney to determine your legal options.

SOLUTION: Respond Appropriately

Different types of citations or deficiencies require different types of responses. Here are some suggestions about how you can frame your response.

VARIANCES

The nature of regulatory language is such that sometimes there is more than one way to meet its intent. Many states give providers the opportunity to apply for a variance. The burden of proof then falls on you to demonstrate how you will comply with the intent, if not the words, of the regulation. An example of this is an Alternate Play Space Agreement. Usually, in order to be licensed, you are required to have a specific amount of usable space inside and outside your home. In most instances, daily outdoor play is a regulatory requirement. For those providers without immediate access to a safe outdoor play area, there is often a provision that allows you to demonstrate alternate ways to provide time outdoors. For instance, you might use the local park or take daily walks in your neighborhood. Know what the options are in your state. When asking about variances, make sure you choose one that will actually work in your program. Don't commit yourself to a variance if you have no realistic way to implement it.

APPEALS

Legal orders usually contain information about an appeal process. When you file an appeal, you are appealing the decision as outlined in the legal order. A legal order is commonly filed only as a result of numerous, or very serious, noncompliances. Read any information provided to you carefully, and get assistance prior to responding if you are confused. If you forgo your right to appeal or you miss the deadline for an appeal, you are likely to end up out of business. Don't let embarrassment keep you from seeking assistance if you need it. Examine your options carefully.

CHALLENGING A CITATION

You usually have the right to challenge individual citations, such as visit reports. If you feel your interpretation of a regulation is accurate and you believe you are not in violation, then you may want to consider challenging the citation. Keep in mind that a valid reason for challenging is not "The licensor wouldn't have caught me if she hadn't dropped by for an unannounced visit." In most states, when you are open for business and caring for children, you are subject to unannounced visits. Do not confuse challenging a regulatory decision with attempting to get even with a regulator.

COMPLAINT INVESTIGATIONS

Complaint investigations are rarely easy. Many providers find it difficult to believe someone would actually report them. In most states, the identity of complainants is confidential. Don't waste your energy trying to find out who filed the complaint. If you are operating your program appropriately, it doesn't matter who filed the complaint, because the investigation will find that the allegations are false. If the allegations are true and the regulator finds evidence to support them, it still makes no difference who filed the complaint. So focus on how quickly you can resolve the problem. If the citation is valid, respond by explaining how you have corrected it. Do not spend time including information about a nosy neighbor or a parent who is trying to get back at you and who you assume filed the complaint. Frankly, no one cares. The regulators' focus is on how quickly you make corrections.

Be careful about your assumptions regarding who filed a complaint. A complaint may be filed by the person you least suspect, someone who actually cares about you and the children enrolled in your program. If you are cited for an obvious noncompliance during a complaint visit, always respond in a manner that reflects your professionalism.

LANGUAGE AND CULTURAL ISSUES

If English is not your primary language and you receive a report that you cannot read, get help. Many agencies employ multilingual staff. You cannot receive assistance if the agencies responsible for visiting your home do not know you need it. Ask for someone who speaks your language to visit. If this is not possible, ask what options are available for translating the materials you are required to read and understand. If the responsible agency is not prepared to offer bilingual personnel or translated materials, you should make arrangements to have someone you know and trust translate for you. This might sound like an undue burden, but the alternative is not a good one. You need to be able to understand what is communicated to you during a visit. You also need to be able to understand the requirements for providing child care and know exactly what your agreement means. This is especially true when responding to reports and citations. Make sure that whoever assists you with translation is able to understand and communicate what is required. Avoid relying on children or individuals who may speak English but cannot read it.

CHALLENGE: Ensuring Information Made Available to the Public Is Correct

How times have changed! It is one thing to deal one-on-one with a regulator. It is an entirely different situation to deal with information posted on the Internet. In some cases, even when noncompliances are corrected immediately, they are slow to actually appear on the site, if at all. If your state has a provision for removing citations when a noncompliance is corrected, this can take much longer than you wish. In some cases, the citation might not be removed at all. What to do?

SOLUTION: Stay Up to Date on How Your State Shares Information

Since each state is different, this book can only provide general guidelines. It is up to you to obtain the specifics relevant to you. However, the following helpful hints should start you on the right path.

If you live in a state where your licensing history is posted on a public website, check the site periodically for accuracy. You can't correct misleading or incorrect information if you don't know it's there. If your state does not currently operate this type of website, periodically call your regulatory authority to review the information it gives to prospective clients who are checking your licensing history.

Be sure to find out how information gets corrected before you actually need to request a correction. Ask your regulator, or send a letter to your regulatory agency requesting the procedure for correcting public information contained in your licensing file.

Make sure you understand the types of information shared with families seeking family child care. For example, if you have a college degree, employ approved assistants, or have your Child Development Associate credential, is that information included in your licensing profile? Positive information creates a good balance for someone reviewing information about your program. Ask, and make sure you include all the positive information about you and your program when you can.

If you read false information about yourself and your business, submit a letter and any other relevant material to demonstrate why the information is incorrect. Be concise—keep your letter to one page, if possible. Give specific information on why the information should not appear as part of your licensing history. Limit your submission to copies of reports that substantiate your claim. This is when your note taking becomes especially important, because you can submit copies of your notes. If they have been signed and dated by the regulator, they will be helpful when you are challenging incorrect information.

Identify the correct department or individual responsible for making corrections to your file. Make sure you keep a copy of any paperwork you submit, and send your information in a way that allows you to track its arrival. If you send your information by e-mail, for example, require an acknowledgment. If you mail information, you may choose to send a certified letter or request a return receipt. Do not be shy about following up with phone calls. Be professional, but be persistent.

Be prepared to be candid with prospective clients during your initial interview. A parent who has reviewed your licensing history might not reveal she has this information; she might be waiting to see what you have to say. It is far better for you to be upfront, discuss any compliance problems you have had, and then explain how those issues have been corrected. If you are in the process of correcting information that was mistakenly included in your file, share that as well. Your goal should be to give a balanced and fair perspective of your licensing history. Share complaint or citation information in the same professional manner you share all the positive information about your program.

CASE STUDY 2:
Kay Is Confident and Knowledgeable

Kay has been providing child care in her home for twenty-eight years. During this time, she has worked hard and has established a good reputation in her community. Not only does Kay always have a waiting list, but she has also earned the respect of her peers. Kay has been a mentor and has sat on state-sponsored committees to examine regulations. She has applied for and earned national accreditation. Kay has a lot of confidence in her ability to operate a successful child care business.

Over the years, Kay has seen many regulators come and go. When she first became licensed, she was very nervous about the periodic inspections necessary to maintain her license and enrollment in the food program. However, she realizes that she often seems better informed about the requirements necessary to operate her business than many of the people visiting her home. On many occasions, she has found herself instructing her regulators. Because of this, Kay recognizes that it is especially important for her to listen carefully and to document what is said during each monitoring visit.

Because of the turnover of staff visiting her home, Kay knows it is important to pay attention to details and carefully read anything sent to her home as a result of a home visit. She knows that if there is incorrect or misleading information contained in a report, she needs to correct that information as quickly as possible. Although Kay is confident in her ability to provide quality child care, she also recognizes her responsibility to stay informed and to comply with existing regulations. When Kay disagrees with something she is told during a monitoring visit, she asks questions to get clarification, and she takes the time to record the information she receives. In addition, Kay always asks the individual conducting the visit to sign and date her own notes.

Recently, Kay's state chose to post its child care providers' licensing information on its public website. The decision was made to give prospective clients an opportunity to view each child care provider's licensing history. When this new initiative was proposed, Kay was one of its biggest supporters. She wanted the people in her community to recognize the difference between good programs and not so good programs. Kay was confident in her position because she was absolutely certain she operated a very good program.

On the first day the posting appeared, Kay immediately went to the site and looked for her information. Because she had kept abreast of her licensing history and had immediately dealt with any issues that arose during monitoring visits, she had no surprises when she reviewed the website. Kay's posted licensing history accurately reflected what Kay already knew. She has taken good care of her child care business, and she now has the pleasure of seeing that reflected in the information contained on the Internet.

Checkpoints for Success

___ I carefully read any report given to me at the conclusion of a visit.

___ I decline to sign any report that includes incorrect information unless I can include my rebuttal.

___ I compare a visit report with my notes to check for any discrepancies.

___ I immediately open and carefully read any report sent to me as a result of a visit.

___ I take note of any and all time lines included in the report.

___ I seek assistance when necessary.

___ As part of my follow-up, I make corrections, respond professionally, and take appropriate action in a timely fashion.

6-21-18